Diseases and Disorders

Heart Disease

by Barbara Sheen

LUCENT BOOKS®

THOMSON

GALE

San Diego • Detroit • New York • San Francisco • Cleveland
New Haven, Conn. • Waterville, Maine • London • Munich

On cover: A heart patient undergoes coronary bypass surgery.

LIBRARY OF CONGRESS CATALOGING-IN-PUBLICATION DATA

Sheen, Barbara.
  Heart disease / by Barbara Sheen.
    p. cm. — (Diseases and disorders)
  Includes bibliographical references.
  Contents: The leading cause of death in America—What is heart disease?—Symptoms and diagnosis—Conventional and alternative treatments—Living with heart disease—What the future holds.
  ISBN 1-59018-347-9
  1. Heart—Diseases—Juvenile literature. I. Title. II. Series: Disease and disorders series.
  RC673.S54 2004
  616.1'2—dc22
                                                                    2004006209

Printed in the United States of America

Table of Contents

"The Most Difficult Puzzles Ever Devised"

CHARLES BEST, ONE of the pioneers in the search for a cure for diabetes, once explained what it is about medical research that intrigued him so. "It's not just the gratification of knowing one is helping people," he confided, "although that probably is a more heroic and selfless motivation. Those feelings may enter in, but truly, what I find best is the feeling of going toe to toe with nature, of trying to solve the most difficult puzzles ever devised. The answers are there somewhere, those keys that will solve the puzzle and make the patient well. But how will those keys be found?"

Since the dawn of civilization, nothing has so puzzled people—and often frightened them, as well—as the onset of illness in a body or mind that had seemed healthy before. A seizure, the inability of a heart to pump, the sudden deterioration of muscle tone in a small child—being unable to reverse such conditions or even to understand why they occur was unspeakably frustrating to healers. Even before there were names for such conditions, even before they were understood at all, each was a reminder of how complex the human body was, and how vulnerable.

While our grappling with understanding diseases has been frustrating at times, it has also provided some of humankind's most heroic accomplishments. Alexander Fleming's accidental discovery in 1928 of a mold that could be turned into penicillin has resulted in the saving of untold millions of lives. The isolation of the enzyme insulin has reversed what was once a death sentence for anyone with diabetes. There have been great strides in combating conditions for which there is not yet a cure, too. Medicines can help AIDS patients live longer, diagnostic tools such as mammography and ultrasounds can help doctors find tumors while they are treatable, and laser surgery techniques have made the most intricate, minute operations routine.

This "toe-to-toe" competition with diseases and disorders is even more remarkable when seen in a historical continuum. An astonishing amount of progress has been made in a very short time. Just two hundred years ago, the existence of germs as a cause of some diseases was unknown. In fact, it was less than 150 years ago that a British surgeon named Joseph Lister had difficulty persuading his fellow doctors that washing their hands before delivering a baby might increase the chances of a healthy delivery (especially if they had just attended to a diseased patient)!

Each book in Lucent's Diseases and Disorders series explores a disease or disorder and the knowledge that has been accumulated (or discarded) by doctors through the years. Each book also examines the tools used for pinpointing a diagnosis, as well as the various means that are used to treat or cure a disease. Finally, new ideas are presented—techniques or medicines that may be on the horizon.

Frustration and disappointment are still part of medicine, for not every disease or condition can be cured or prevented. But the limitations of knowledge are being pushed outward constantly; the "most difficult puzzles ever devised" are finding challengers every day.

The Leading Cause of Death in America

KAYLA IS A college student and star athlete. Steve is a middle-aged school administrator. Perry is a senior citizen. Aaron is an elementary school student. Madison is a toddler. On the surface, these five people appear to have little in common. Yet each of these individuals, like 60 million other Americans, suffers from some type of heart disease.

About one in four Americans has heart disease, and half of these people do not know they have it. This is because heart disease often develops gradually, with no noticeable warning signs, and remains undetected until a heart attack strikes, which happens quite frequently in people with heart disease. In fact, 50 percent of women and 63 percent of men who suffer a fatal heart attack have no previous symptoms of heart disease.

In the United States, 1 million people have heart attacks each year: about one person every twenty seconds. In 44 percent of cases, the result is death. Indeed, heart disease is the leading cause of death in the United States. It kills more people than cancer, all accidents, and HIV combined. Approximately 42 percent of Americans die as a result of heart disease. That translates to about one hundred heart disease–related deaths every hour.

Denying the Problem

Complicating matters, although heart disease strikes both males and females of every age, race, and fitness level, many people believe that heart disease is typically a disease of elderly, physically unfit men. Therefore, younger, physically fit people often ignore heart attack symptoms, mistakenly believing they cannot be afflicted with heart disease. That is what happened to Fred, a heart attack survivor. "A life-threatening illness was unthinkable to me at the time," he explains. "I was 45 years old, at the top of my career, having the time of my life. . . . At the time I was bicycling 10 miles a day and feeling great . . . couldn't be having a [heart attack]. I wouldn't allow myself to consider the words."[1]

Fred waited about twelve hours from the time his heart attack began before seeking help, and this is not uncommon. Half of all heart attack victims wait two or more hours before seeking help. Some people wait days before seeking treatment. For example, Marie started feeling pain in her back and arms while she was working in her home. An article in the October 2003 issue of *Good Housekeeping* quotes her: "I thought I needed a break." The article goes on to explain, "Over the next few days, the pressure intensified. It was there when she typed, made dinner, played with her sons. 'I was scared,' she says. When she finally called her doctor, he urged her to get to the hospital. There, she learned she'd had a minor heart attack."[2]

Such delays can be dangerous. When it comes to a heart attack, every minute treatment is delayed increases the victim's risk of suffering long-term heart damage—or even death. But because heart disease often has no early symptoms, and because many people do not think a heart attack can happen to them, many people put themselves at risk. In fact, at least 250,000 Americans suffering heart attacks each year die before they reach the hospital.

A Disease That Affects Everyone

Heart disease affects many people. It is not a problem just for individuals who have it, but also for their families and friends, and for society. In fact, it would be hard to find anyone in the United States who does not know someone with heart disease.

Economically, the national impact of heart disease is staggering: It exceeds $286 billion a year. This sum includes the cost of health care, medication, and lost productivity. In the state of Utah alone, daily the cost of hospital care for people with heart disease exceeds five hundred thousand dollars. Moreover, many people living with heart disease are unable to work. For example, 73 percent of healthy people between the ages of fifty-one and sixty-

Because many people believe that only elderly or physically unfit men suffer from heart disease, they often dismiss characteristic symptoms of heart attack, such as backache or arm pain.

one are currently in the workforce, but only 48 percent of those fifty-one- to sixty-one-year-olds with heart disease are able to work. Many of these people and their families are forced to collect disability or public assistance, which is paid for through taxes.

Becoming Informed

Because the impact of heart disease is so far-reaching, it is important that people learn more about it. Understanding what causes the disease and what lifestyle factors put people at risk may help many people to avoid or delay the onset of heart disease. Learning about the symptoms of a heart attack and how a heart attack is treated may save many lives. Moreover, knowledge about heart disease can help patients and their families learn better ways to cope with the challenges they face. Max, a heart attack survivor, explains: "I thought I was fairly sophisticated for a lay person . . . but I quickly discovered the shortcomings of my understanding. I began to appreciate just how crucial health information is to improving one's chances of survival and/or enhancing the quality of life."[3]

Chapter 1

What Is Heart Disease?

HEART DISEASE IS a term used to describe a number of different problems that affect the heart's ability to pump blood to the body. Some people are born with heart disease, known as congenital heart disease. However, most cases of heart disease occur later in life. Such cases are called coronary heart disease or coronary artery disease.

Congenital Heart Disease

Congenital heart disease occurs when a fetus's heart fails to develop normally. It affects forty-four thousand babies born in the United States each year, making it the most common of all birth defects. Since the heart is one of the first organs to develop in a fetus, it is especially vulnerable to damage during the first twelve weeks of a woman's pregnancy. Unfortunately, during this time many women are unaware that they are pregnant and may expose themselves to dangerous chemicals that can affect the development of the fetus's heart. Exposure to the rubella, or German measles, virus can also damage the fetus's heart. So, too, can genetic abnormalities. But even when none of these factors are present, congenital heart disease may still occur. In fact, scientists are unable to determine the cause of almost half of all cases of congenital heart disease.

No matter the cause, babies born with congenital heart disease may have any number of defects in the heart and the large blood vessels connected to the heart. Of the thirty-five different types of congenital heart defects, the most common problem is a hole in the heart, which makes up 50 percent of all cases of congenital heart disease. This is a hole between the chambers of the heart, which causes too much blood to flow from the heart to the lungs, making it difficult for the infant to breathe.

Other problems occur when the blood vessels that carry blood to and from the heart are reversed. This causes the body to receive deoxygenated blood, or blood without oxygen, rather than the oxygenated blood the body needs to survive. Abnormalities in the valves that control the flow of blood into and out of the heart are also commonly found in infants with congenital heart disease. These valves may not be able to open or close properly, or the valve openings may be too narrow, forcing the heart to work harder than normal to push blood through.

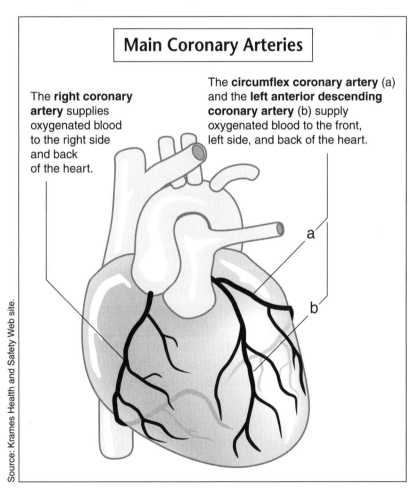

Main Coronary Arteries

The **right coronary artery** supplies oxygenated blood to the right side and back of the heart.

The **circumflex coronary artery** (a) and the **left anterior descending coronary artery** (b) supply oxygenated blood to the front, left side, and back of the heart.

a

b

Fortunately, some congenital heart defects are so mild that they resolve on their own, and advances in science mean most others are treatable. Indeed, most infants with congenital heart disease go on to live normal, happy lives. Anna Jaworski, the mother of a child with congenital heart disease, explains: "Children with heart defects are attending day care, going to school or college and joining the work force. . . . Children with congenital heart disease might attend the same school as your children do. They go to local churches. They ride their bikes, roller blade and play some sports, just like any other child."[4]

Coronary Heart Disease

Unlike congenital heart disease, coronary heart disease develops gradually over a number of years. It is usually the result of blockages in any of the three main coronary arteries or their branches, all of which supply blood to the heart. Problems arise because the heart, which acts as a central pump for the whole body, needs a large and constant supply of oxygenated blood in order to function properly. With every beat, oxygenated blood enters the left side of the heart through the coronary arteries. The heart uses approximately one-quarter of the oxygenated blood itself and pumps the rest to other tissues throughout the body. Once all the oxygen has been extracted from the blood, veins carry the deoxygenated blood back to the right side of the heart, which pumps it to the lungs, where it gets more oxygen. Then the reoxygenated blood travels back to the left side of the heart and the cycle begins again.

Valves on each section of the heart act as one-way doors that keep the blood from flowing in the wrong direction. At the same time, electrical impulses keep the heart beating at the proper pace. Cardiologist and author Seth Baum explains: "Our hearts are fed by blood, just as our cars are fueled by gas—but the spark that begins each heartbeat is an electrical one. The heart possesses a complex electrical network of electrical 'wires' which rapidly disseminate a single spark resulting in a heart beat."[5]

With each beat, the heart either contracts or relaxes. Each contraction pushes blood into the arteries. When a person is at rest, the heart beats about 70 times per minute. But when a person is exercising and the body needs more blood and oxygen, the heart may beat more than 180 times per minute. However, if the coronary arteries become blocked, the heart's ability to pump blood becomes impaired and the heart's supply of oxygenated blood is reduced.

Cholesterol Causes Problems

A number of factors can cause the coronary arteries to become blocked. Scientists have not yet determined what they all may be. Scientists do know that cholesterol plays an important role. Cholesterol is a waxy fat that is manufactured by the liver, and it is also found in foods such as meat, eggs, and dairy products. Among other things, the body needs cholesterol to build cell walls and to form a protective coating around nerves.

In order to do its job, cholesterol must travel through the bloodstream. But like any fat, cholesterol cannot dissolve in liquid, which it would need to do to move through the bloodstream alone. To solve this problem, cholesterol wraps itself around proteins known as lipoproteins, whose function it is to carry cholesterol and other fats through the body.

Lipoproteins are classified into two main types: high-density and low-density lipoproteins. As the name implies, high-density lipoproteins, or HDLs, are quite dense. They are also firm and difficult to adhere to. On average, one-quarter to one-third of lipoproteins found in the human body are high-density lipoproteins. Low-density lipoproteins, or LDLs, make up two-thirds to three-quarters of all lipoproteins. Low-density lipoproteins are soft and tend to be sticky. Therefore, it is not surprising that bits of low-density lipoproteins often get stuck to cell walls.

Each type of lipoprotein does its job differently. LDLs pick up cholesterol in the liver and transport it to sites all over the body, including the coronary arteries. HDLs roam through the body picking up excess cholesterol that the body cannot use. The HDLs transport this excess cholesterol back to the liver, where it is processed and eliminated from the body. This protects the body from the damage excess cholesterol can cause. Even though HDLs are not actually cholesterol, they are commonly called "good cholesterol" because they carry cholesterol away from the coronary arteries.

Source: Krames Health and Safety Web site.

Fatty Deposit Buildup in an Artery

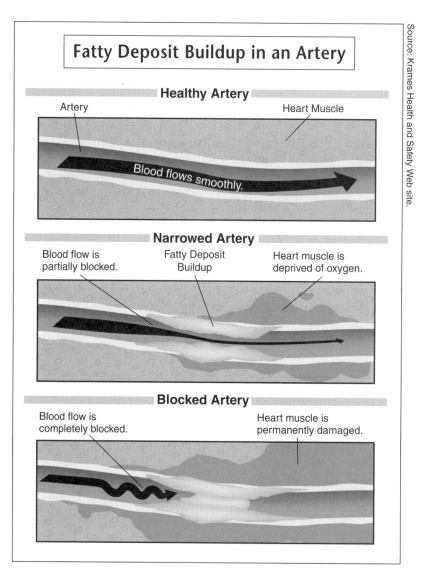

Healthy Artery

Artery

Heart Muscle

Blood flows smoothly.

Narrowed Artery

Blood flow is partially blocked.

Fatty Deposit Buildup

Heart muscle is deprived of oxygen.

Blocked Artery

Blood flow is completely blocked.

Heart muscle is permanently damaged.

Problems arise when too many LDLs circulate in the blood, making it impossible for the HDLs to gather all the excess cholesterol. When this happens, excess cholesterol is deposited in the coronary arteries, which are easy to adhere to because they are wide and smooth. As these fatty deposits build up, they clog the coronary arteries and slow the flow of blood. This is why LDLs are known as "bad cholesterol."

Making matters worse, because LDL deposits are sticky, substances in the bloodstream such as calcium, white blood cells, and a type of red blood cell called platelets get stuck to the fatty deposits when they pass through the artery. When these substances mix with cholesterol, a chemical reaction causes them to harden, forming a rough substance called plaque. As more cholesterol is sent into the bloodstream, plaque deposits grow. As a result, the passageway continues to narrow, and blood flow to the heart becomes progressively slower and more difficult. This is known as atherosclerosis.

Dangerous Blood Clots

Complicating matters, plaque is hard and rough, and it scratches and cracks the smooth walls of the coronary arteries. In an effort to heal the damaged artery walls, the immune system sends additional white blood cells and platelets to the artery, where they form fibrous clots over the plaque. However, as the plaque deposit grows, damage to the artery walls recurs. This process continuously repeats itself and new blood clots form over the old blood clots. Eventually, the blood clots may become so large that they completely block blood flow. This is known as a thrombosis.

Even when a blood clot does not become big enough to block the artery, other trouble can arise. Blood clots of any size can break off of a plaque deposit. The blood clot may be carried through the coronary artery until it lodges inside a tiny blood vessel called a capillary, which is part of a network of blood vessels connecting to the coronary arteries. Because capillaries are extremely small and narrow, blood clots can easily get stuck in them, keeping blood from reaching the coronary arteries and the heart.

When the heart's ability to pump blood becomes compromised, whether due to congenital heart defects, atherosclerosis, or a thrombosis, the result is always heart disease. If it is not effectively controlled, heart disease can lead to heart attacks and death.

People at Risk

Anyone can get heart disease. However, certain groups of people are most at risk. Babies whose mothers are exposed to powerful

Babies whose mothers are exposed to powerful chemicals during pregnancy, such as cleaning fluids and pesticides, are at a high risk of developing a congenital heart defect.

chemicals, including industrial-strength cleaning fluids and pesticides, during the first trimester of pregnancy are a high-risk group. In fact, according to the Heart Center Online, a source of information about heart disease for patients and doctors, pregnant women exposed to rat poison are six times more likely than women not exposed to this pesticide to have a child born with a congenital heart defect. Such problems occur because any chemical an expectant mother ingests, whether through the mouth or the lungs, enters the mother's bloodstream and is passed to the fetus through the placenta.

Other chemicals also put infants at risk. These include alcohol and other recreational drugs such as cocaine and heroin. Alcohol in particular appears to affect the development of a fetus's heart. According to the March of Dimes, babies born with fetal alcohol syndrome, a condition caused by a fetus's exposure to alcohol, often have congenital heart problems.

Genetics

Genetics, too, influences an infant's risk of congenital heart disease. Although scientists have not yet identified a particular gene that causes the heart to develop abnormally, they do know that people with congenital heart disease have a higher risk of having a child with the condition. In fact, according to the American Heart Association, a baby with one parent with congenital heart disease has up to a 20 percent chance of also having a heart defect, and with each additional close family member who is affected, the baby's risk increases. A mother with a mild congenital heart defect known as a heart murmur explains how this risk factor affected her son, Travis: "I watched as the doctor listened to his heart; he was listening too long. When he finally faced my husband and me, he explained that Travis had a murmur. I feverishly explained that I too had a murmur."[6]

Similarly, genetics appears to play a role in the development of coronary heart disease. The more close relatives a person has with coronary heart disease, the more likely that person is to develop it. This is especially true if the relative developed coronary heart disease at an early age. Experts say such early development may indicate a genetic tendency for plaque to build up more rapidly than usual. In fact, the editors of *A Healthy Heart* report that if a person's father has a heart attack before age fifty, or his or her mother has a heart attack before age sixty-five, that person's chance of developing coronary heart disease quadruples. Therefore, it is not surprising that most experts consider a family history of heart disease the single greatest risk factor for developing coronary heart disease.

Once again, scientists have not identified a specific gene that causes this, but theorize that a combination of mutant genes predispose certain people to produce excess LDLs and plaque. Jacob, a coronary heart disease patient, describes how genetics affected him: "My great-grandfather and my grandfather both died of heart attacks, and my father had a heart attack at age 63. . . . I had a strong history of heart disease on my father's side of the family, from which I probably inherited these genetic problems."[7]

Elevated Cholesterol

Having elevated blood cholesterol, whether due to genetics or a diet high in animal fats, is another factor that puts people at risk. According to the American Heart Association, total cholesterol, which is typically measured in milligrams per deciliter of blood, should be no more than two hundred. People with levels greater than two hundred are at risk of developing coronary heart disease. John, a man with high cholesterol, explains: "My cholesterol was over three hundred. I didn't think it was a big deal. But the doctor thought otherwise. He said something had to be done about it before I keeled over with a heart attack."[8]

The American Heart Association says HDL levels should be forty or above, while LDLs should be less than one hundred. The higher a person's level of LDLs, the more danger he or she has of developing atherosclerosis. Conversely, high levels of HDLs appear to lower a person's risk of developing atherosclerosis, since HDLs reduce some of the harmful effects of LDLs. Low levels of HDLs increase a person's risk of developing atherosclerosis.

Age and Gender

Age and gender are other factors that influence an individual's risk of developing coronary heart disease. Males are five times more likely to develop coronary heart disease than are females who have not yet reached menopause. This is because before menopause females produce high levels of the hormone estrogen, which men do not. Although scientists do not know why, high levels of estrogen appear to encourage the production of HDLs, which help the body eliminate excess cholesterol. This changes after a woman reaches menopause, normally sometime around fifty years of age, when a woman's estrogen production decreases considerably. In addition,

Premenopausal women produce high levels of estrogen that help reduce cholesterol. Estrogen production drops during menopause, however, increasing the risk of heart disease.

a number of studies have shown that the risk of coronary heart disease increases for both men and women as they age. This is because as people age, plaque deposits gradually build up until they cause problems. Indeed, according to the American Heart Association, an individual's risk of developing coronary heart disease increases every ten years. So it is not surprising that more than half of all heart attack patients are at least sixty-five years old, or that 84 percent of all deaths from heart disease occur in people over sixty-five.

High Blood Pressure

High blood pressure is another risk factor. As the heart pumps blood, the blood creates pressure in the arteries, making the artery walls expand. This pressure is referred to as blood pressure.

People with high blood pressure are at risk for heart disease. High blood pressure causes the heart to work harder than normal, often leading to significant coronary damage.

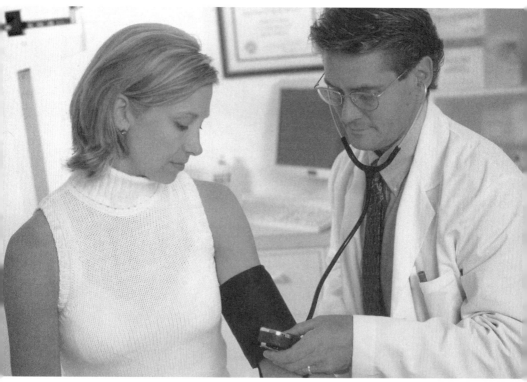

Blood pressure is measured in millimeters and stated as two numbers. The top number indicates the pressure exerted as the heart contracts, and the bottom number signifies the pressure when the heart relaxes. Normal blood pressure is typically about 120/80. Numbers above this indicate hypertension, or high blood pressure. High blood pressure causes the heart to pump faster and with more force than normal in order to push the blood through the arteries. Over time, this damages and weakens the heart. In addition, high blood pressure is frequently responsible for causing small blood clots to break loose and clog capillaries.

Smoking

Because smoking raises blood pressure, people who smoke are at risk of developing heart disease. Nicotine, a powerful chemical found in tobacco, damages the walls of the coronary arteries, causing them to narrow. As a result, blood pressure rises and the heart must pump harder. Although scientists are not sure why, nicotine also seems to cause HDL levels to fall.

Indeed, according to the American Heart Association, smoking triples a person's risk of developing heart disease. Therefore, it is not surprising that Seth Baum reports that males who smoke at least ten cigarettes a day increase their risk of dying from coronary heart disease by 18 percent, while females increase their risk by 31 percent. Fred Abatemarco explains how smoking put him at risk: "I was a prime candidate. Though I may have seemed like a healthy man, the warning signs were there—if I'd cared to notice. . . . I had smoked cigarettes since my teen years. Though I quit them more than a decade before, I remained a nicotine addict gratified by cigars."[9]

Stress

People who are under chronic stress are also at risk of developing heart disease. Stress causes the heart to beat faster and blood pressure to rise. It also causes the body to produce cortisol and adrenalin, the so-called fight-or-flight hormones. These hormones stimulate the liver to manufacture excess cholesterol in an effort to provide the body with energy to fight the stressor. When stress is temporary, the body quickly reverts to normal. However, when

Because stress causes the heart to beat faster and elevates blood pressure, people under chronic stress are at high risk of developing heart complications.

stress is persistent, these factors do not go away, and the person's risk of developing heart disease rises.

"I think stress caused my heart attack," explains Perry, a heart attack survivor. "I didn't have any of the risk factors, not genetics, neither my father or mother had a heart attack; not high blood pressure, or high cholesterol. But there were lots of problems at my job, lots of problems. My two predecessors at that job both got heart attacks, too."[10]

Physical Inactivity

Physical inactivity is still another risk factor. The heart is composed of muscle fiber. As it does with any other muscle, exercise strengthens the heart. As a consequence, active people's hearts are stronger and do not have to work as hard as the hearts of people who are inactive. In fact, because the hearts of active people are stronger, they beat more slowly than the hearts of inactive people, even at rest. Conversely, an inactive person's heart is less efficient and has to work harder to pump adequate blood to the body. Over time, this can weaken the heart.

Can Heart Disease Be Prevented?

Since it is impossible to change certain risk factors such as age, gender, and genetics, heart disease cannot always be prevented. However, by eliminating as many risk factors as possible, people can reduce their chance of developing heart disease. Avoiding dangerous chemicals during pregnancy can help a pregnant woman lower her baby's risk of congenital heart disease. Lowering stress, blood pressure, and cholesterol; being physically active; and not smoking can all reduce a person's risk of developing coronary heart disease. Indeed, research indicates that making such changes can substantially lower a person's risk. The Framingham Heart Study is a fifty-four-year-long ongoing study that has followed 5,209 adult residents of Framingham, Massachusetts, to learn the circumstances in which heart disease develops. The study found that having one risk factor doubles a person's risk of developing heart disease. With two risk factors, the risk quadruples, and with three risk factors, the risk increases anywhere from eight to twenty times. Although there is no way to guarantee that an individual will not develop heart disease, reducing risk factors can help tremendously. John explains: "Heart disease runs in my family. I can't change that. But I'm working at lowering my cholesterol, and I exercise every day. Hopefully, it will keep my heart healthy."[11]

It is clear that heart disease is a serious condition. But by lessening modifiable risk factors, people like John can reduce their chances of developing heart disease.

Chapter 2

Symptoms and Diagnosis

Diagnosing congenital heart disease is not difficult. This is especially true of many congenital heart defects with well-defined symptoms. Usually the skin, fingernails, and lips of infants with congenital heart disease have a bluish tinge. Since oxygenated blood is red in color and deoxygenated blood appears blue when viewed through the skin, a bluish color indicates that not enough oxygenated blood is being pumped to the body.

Decreased blood flow to the lungs causes many babies with congenital heart defects to have problems breathing. Consequently, most cases are diagnosed at birth or shortly thereafter. The mother of Matthew, a baby with congenital heart disease, explains:

> About an hour after Matthew was born, a nurse noticed Matthew's respiration was high. . . . About 10:30 the next morning, a nurse noticed Matthew looked bluish. . . . About midnight two days later the neonatologist [a doctor who cares for newborn babies] told us Matthew wasn't responding to any lung medication, so they were going to test his heart. . . . Matthew's tests indicated heart problems.[12]

The symptoms of coronary heart disease are not quite as distinct and take decades to develop. This is because in some—but not all—people, the outer walls of the coronary arteries adapt to the buildup of plaque by expanding. This allows blood to reach the heart. Therefore, many people with coronary heart disease remain undiagnosed until the coronary artery, which can expand only so far, becomes completely blocked with plaque or a blood clot, causing a heart attack. That is what happened to Perry: "I didn't know what was wrong. I didn't think it was a heart attack. I was sixty years old. My cholesterol was low. I never had any heart problems. I just knew something was wrong, real wrong."[13]

Different Symptoms for Different Problems

Some people do complain of specific symptoms that indicate coronary heart disease. The most common symptom is temporary chest

Congenital heart disease is typically diagnosed in infancy. Babies with congenital heart disease have trouble breathing, and their skin, lips, and fingernails have a bluish tinge.

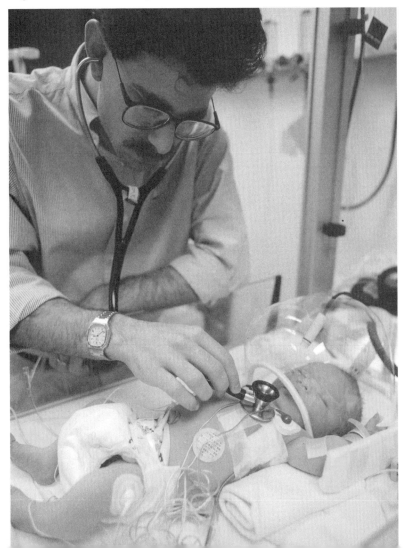

pain known as angina, which literally means a choking sensation in the chest. Angina occurs whenever the heart receives insufficient oxygen-rich blood due to atherosclerosis. Angina pain is usually brought on when the heart requires more blood than normal, such as during physical exertion or stress, but because of clogged arteries the demand for extra blood cannot be met. This causes temporary chest pain that usually subsides when the heart's demand for blood returns to normal. Marilyn explains: "I have angina. I get it sometimes when I'm walking in the wind. It's a pain under my breastbone, like in my rib section. It's not too bad. It always goes away when I get inside and sit down and rest." [14]

More than 6 million Americans suffer from angina. In general, angina pain lasts less than ten minutes. However, if blockages become severe and oxygenated blood can no longer reach the heart, angina pain does not subside, even while at rest. When this occurs and chest pain is prolonged rather than temporary, the symptoms point to a heart attack.

Heart Attack

When a heart attack occurs, the heart, even at rest, cannot get blood and oxygen. Like every organ in the body, the heart is fed by oxygenated blood and cannot survive without it. Consequently, when its supply of oxygenated blood is cut off, heart tissue dies.

In an effort to force blood through and keep heart tissue from dying, the clogged arteries may spasm. This, combined with lack of blood and oxygen, causes victims to experience prolonged angina-like pain in their chests, which often radiates to the jaw, neck, left arm, and left shoulder, the side of the body where the heart is located. In some people, the pain may be fairly mild and has been described as a persistent feeling of pressure or tightness. "It was an ordinary evening about four years ago, when I experienced the first twinge of chest pressure," Fred Abatemarco recalls. "The pain was nowhere near the 'elephant sitting on my chest' description given by some heart-attack victims. It felt more like heartburn. I thought I was coming down with the flu. I went to bed early. But the uneasiness nagged on. The tightening in my chest kept waking me up. . . . At 4 A.M. I began to worry seriously." [15]

Prolonged chest pain is a sure sign of heart attack. Often the pain radiates from the chest to the jaw, neck, left arm, and left shoulder.

Other patients experience more intense pain, which they describe as crushing or burning. Perry remembers: "It was three in the morning and I woke my wife and told her to take me to the emergency room. She thought I had indigestion and didn't want to go. But I knew it wasn't indigestion. With indigestion the pain doesn't hurt and burn in your neck and shoulder and arm. It was bad, real bad."[16]

Prolonged chest pain, whether mild or severe, points to a heart attack. Often, the pain is combined with feelings of light-headedness, nausea, and dizziness, which result from limited blood flow to the brain and stomach. But no matter the symptoms, when the heart's supply of oxygenated blood is cut off, heart tissue gradually starves and dies.

The extent of the damage depends on how much tissue is affected and where the dead tissue is located. Interestingly, in most cases not all of the heart is affected. Each coronary artery supplies blood to a different section of the heart, and only tissue in the part of the heart fed by the blocked artery dies. Of course, if more than one artery is blocked or a large section of the heart depends on the blocked artery for oxygenated blood, the damage will be extensive. In every case, the death of heart tissue is permanent. Worse still, if too much tissue dies before blood flow to the heart can be restored, the heart may be unable to pump blood to the brain or other vital organs. The result is death. According to the American Heart Association, more than 440,000 Americans die of heart attacks each year.

A heart weakened by an attack is forced to work hard to pump sufficient blood throughout the body. As a result, even simple tasks such as dressing can be exhausting.

Other Symptoms Point to Heart Failure

Even when a heart attack is not fatal, the death of heart tissue weakens the heart. So, too, does any condition that causes the heart to work harder, such as some congenital heart defects, as well as atherosclerosis. Since a weak heart is unable to pump as much blood as a healthy heart, blood flow throughout the body is reduced. Therefore, the heart has to work harder to get blood to the body, and this increased workload further weakens the heart. Often the heart may become so weak that it is unable to pump blood well enough to meet the body's needs. Sometimes the heart can pump only 15 percent, rather than the normal 85 percent, of the oxygenated blood to the body. This condition, which affects approximately 5 million Americans, is known as heart failure, or congestive heart failure.

As a consequence of heart failure, patients feel weak, and sometimes unable to perform even small tasks such as getting dressed without becoming exhausted. Moreover, when the heart is unable to pump adequately, water and salt, which are ordinarily carried in the blood, often accumulate in the feet, ankles, stomach, and lungs. Fluid in the lungs causes breathing problems. Max talks about the symptoms he experienced after his heart attack:

> In the winter of 1998 I came down with a severe respiratory infection. . . . I called my doctor for an antibiotic prescription. He gave me the prescription, but insisted I get an X ray of my lungs. He called the next day to tell me the X ray showed fluid in my lungs, a symptom of congestive heart failure. . . . I had known I had a damaged heart, but now I learned that it was becoming less efficient. [17]

Those are not the only symptoms. Depending on which organs are receiving inadequate blood, other problems may arise. For example, if the brain receives inadequate blood, the patient will have trouble thinking clearly. If blood flow to the kidneys is affected, they may fail. Moreover, if the heart continues to weaken and lose its ability to pump blood to the vital organs, the patient will die. Thirty-nine thousand Americans die of heart failure each year.

Erratic Heartbeat

Other troubles arise because of problems in the heart's electrical system. Such troubles can cause an arrhythmia, a condition in which the heart beats too quickly or too slowly in an erratic, unsynchronized manner.

Some arrhythmias are temporary. Many people experience a temporary arrhythmia when they are angry or stressed. They feel like their heart is racing. But this type of arrhythmia corrects itself as the person relaxes and it is harmless.

On the other hand, when the heart's electrical system has been damaged by a heart attack or congenital heart disease, a prolonged and dangerous arrhythmia may result. An arrhythmia often causes the heart to pause, or skip a beat. This is frequently described as a fluttering sensation. It can also cause the heart to beat too slowly, resulting in insufficient blood being pumped to the body. When this happens, the brain may not get enough oxygenated blood, which leads to fatigue and dizziness. This also causes people to faint and fall for no apparent reason.

When a person's heartbeat increases, excess blood is sent to the heart in order to feed it. If the heart beats too quickly, it cannot contract rapidly enough to push the excess blood into the arteries. As a consequence, blood that is meant for the body floods the heart instead, making the heart pound and sometimes causing angina-like chest pains. "I woke up one night with my heart thumping wildly and my chest hurting," an arrhythmia sufferer recalls:

> Just as I was about to reach for the phone, the symptoms passed. I talked to my doctor the next day to see if it was something I should be worried about. He assured me it could be due to lack of sleep or stress or a variety of things, but that it would be a good idea for me to come in and get checked out. . . . [A test] revealed potentially life-threatening information: I had atrial fibrillation [a type of arrhythmia]. [18]

If the heart's normal rhythm is not restored, it may be fatal. Death caused by an abnormal heart rhythm, known as cardiac arrest, affects five hundred thousand people in the United States each year.

Testing

When a person reports any heart disease–related symptoms, heart disease is suspected. However, other conditions such as indigestion, heartburn, bronchitis, asthma, and viral and bacterial infections such as the flu or pneumonia can also cause chest pain, fatigue, and breathing problems. Doctors must administer a number of tests to ascertain that the problem is heart disease and to determine what part of the heart is affected. Tests for heart disease include a physical exam, a blood test, an echocardiogram, an electrocardiogram, a stress test, and an angiogram.

The Physical Exam

Although a physical exam is used to diagnose almost every disease, it is particularly important in diagnosing heart disease. During a physical exam, the doctor takes the patient's pulse; if it is too

The battery of tests performed during a routine physical exam is extremely beneficial in detecting symptoms of heart disease.

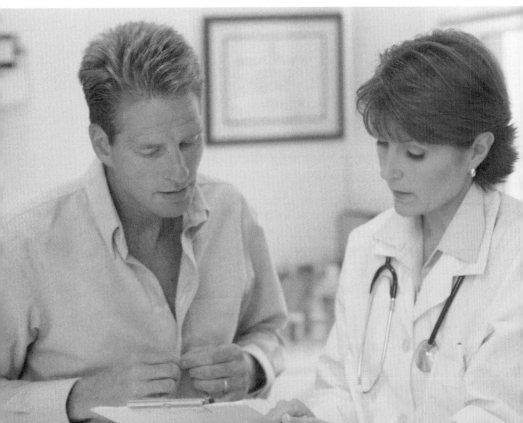

fast or slow, an arrhythmia is indicated. In addition, the doctor often feels the pulse in the two carotid arteries, one on each side of the neck, that carry blood to the brain. If the carotid arteries are pulsing strongly, the doctor knows that there are no blockages in the coronary arteries that feed them. A weak pulse indicates a blockage.

Since high blood pressure often accompanies heart disease, the patient's blood pressure is also checked during the physical exam. The doctor also listens to the sounds the heart makes using a stethoscope. Normally, the doctor hears two sounds known as S1 and S2, which are the sounds of blood leaving the heart as it contracts and relaxes. These sounds, which scientists describe as "lub" and "dub," indicate that blood is being pumped out of the heart without any problems. When these do not sound the way they should, it is often because the heart valves are not functioning correctly and blood is being pushed backward rather than out through the coronary arteries. These sounds help doctors diagnose congenital heart defects as well as heart failure.

In addition, other aspects of the physical exam, such as the patient's temperature, can help the doctor eliminate the possibility of illnesses such as bronchitis or a viral or bacterial infection, which often are accompanied by fever.

Blood Tests

A blood test, too, helps doctors eliminate the possibility of bronchitis or a viral or bacterial infection. A blood test can easily detect elevated white blood cell levels that indicate infection. A high level of red blood cells, on the other hand, indicates a lack of oxygen in the blood, which is often due to congenital or coronary heart disease. Examining gases in the blood helps doctors eliminate other problems. A high level of carbon dioxide, for example, indicates problems in the lungs, such as asthma or bronchitis.

A blood test also helps the doctor determine what is wrong in the heart. A blood fat profile, for instance, measures high- and low-density lipoproteins in the blood. Elevated LDLs are often an indicator of atherosclerosis. Similarly, measuring cardiac enzymes, proteins the heart produces in response to damage, can also pinpoint specific problems. During a heart attack, the heart produces

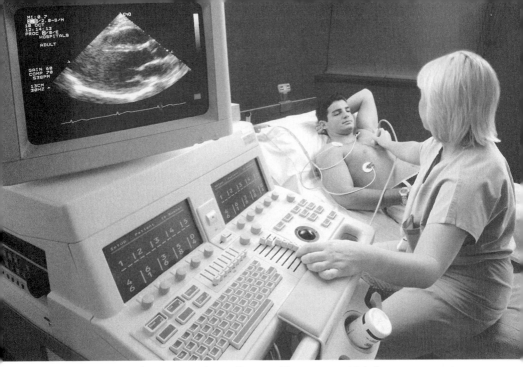

A patient undergoes an echocardiogram. The test uses high-frequency sound waves to produce a detailed picture of the flow of blood through the heart and its valves.

high levels of enzymes in an effort to heal damaged heart tissue. Therefore, when a blood test shows elevated cardiac enzymes, the doctor knows that a heart attack is occurring or has recently occurred. The higher the cardiac enzyme level, the greater the damage. A heart attack survivor explains: "I went into the emergency room and they took me right in. I was like WOW and then reality hit. I had been having a heart attack and the blood test was about to reveal it. Enzymes? What are they? I got an education on my heart."[19]

The Echocardiogram

Another test that helps doctors diagnose damage to the heart, congenital heart defects, disorders of the heart valves, blood flow problems, and heart failure is an echocardiogram. This test, also referred to as an ultrasound, uses high-frequency sound waves to obtain a picture of the heart.

During an echocardiogram the patient lies on a table where a conductive gel that improves the transmission of sound waves is rubbed on his or her chest. Then a small handheld device called a transducer is passed across the patient's chest. The transducer, which is attached to a computer, emits high-frequency sound waves. The sound waves bounce back from the heart to the computer, which interprets the pattern of the sound waves and converts them to pictures. The pictures appear on a computer monitor. The echocardiogram gives the doctor a detailed picture of the heart and the blood flow through the heart and its valves. This makes it easy for the doctor to see how well the heart is pumping, whether heart tissue is damaged or dead, whether there are congenital defects such as a hole in the heart, and whether blood is flowing adequately through the valves.

Sometimes an echocardiogram can help save a patient's life. Noah, a baby with breathing problems, was misdiagnosed with pneumonia. An echocardiogram, however, showed that his real problem was congenital heart failure. An article appearing on the Kansas City Community Blood Center Web site explains: "His x-ray showed fluid in his lungs. . . . An echocardiogram determined that Noah had a very serious heart defect. The fluid in his lungs

A nurse monitors a patient's blood pressure during an exercise stress test. The test allows the doctor to evaluate how the heart responds to the stresses of physical activity.

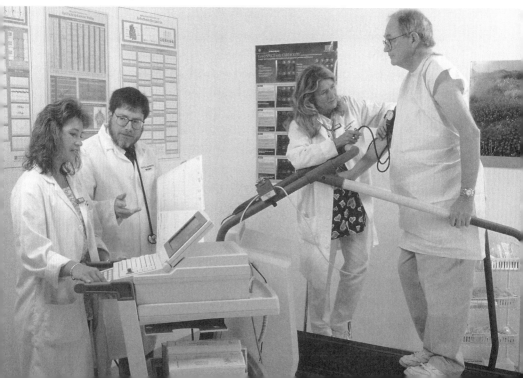

was not from pneumonia, but was caused by congestive heart failure. At 9:30 the next morning, Noah underwent an emergency operation to repair his damaged heart and save his life." [20]

The Electrocardiogram

An electrocardiogram, or EKG, is quite similar to an echocardiogram. However, instead of sound waves, electricity is used to evaluate the amount of time it takes an electrical wave to go across the heart while the heart is at rest. The results help the doctor assess electrical activity within the heart in order to diagnose an arrhythmia, blocked blood flow, damaged and dead heart tissue, and certain congenital heart defects.

During an EKG, twelve small pads, or electrodes, which are connected by wires to an electrocardiograph machine, are placed on the patient's chest, arms, and legs. The patient lies still for two minutes while each electrode measures electrical activity in a different part of the heart and adjoining arteries. The findings are interpreted simultaneously by a computer and produced in the form of a graph. Abnormalities in the graph alert the doctor to heart problems.

The Stress Test

Since an EKG is given while a patient is at rest, some heart problems that usually emerge only when a person is under stress, such as angina and problems in the heart valves, may not be apparent during an EKG. In fact, according to the Heart Center Online, a resting EKG is inaccurate 50 percent of the time. In order to compare the heart's electrical activity when it is at rest to that when it is under stress, and to better diagnose stress-related abnormalities, a special type of electrocardiogram may be administered.

This test, known as an exercise stress test, is administered in a similar fashion to a resting EKG, but rather than lying still, the patient exercises on a treadmill or stationary bike at increasing speeds and elevations for about fifteen minutes. This enables the doctor to measure how the patient's heart responds to physical stress as well as the heart's ability to pump blood. In addition, spikes in blood pressure and blockages in the coronary arteries appear as abnormalities on the graph.

Throughout the test, the patient's blood pressure and heart rate are carefully monitored, and if the patient complains of any chest pain or has trouble breathing, the test is ended. Marilyn describes her experience: "They attached electrodes to me. Then they put me on a treadmill. First, they made it go slow and then it went a little faster. Gradually, it went faster and faster. When it went too fast and I was tired, they stopped the thing and took me off of it."[21]

The Angiogram

When a stress test indicates blocked blood flow, still another test, called an angiogram, is often administered. This test allows the doctor to pinpoint the exact location of blockages and to determine the extent of the blockage. It involves the threading of a tiny plastic tube, called a catheter, into an artery in the patient's groin and then up to the coronary arteries. Dye is injected into the catheter, and the path of the dye is monitored via X-ray. In this manner, blockages in the coronary arteries and their network of capillaries can easily be located and analyzed. Hans recalls his experience: "The cardiologist took a coronary angiogram. It showed a complete blockage of the left anterior descending artery [a coronary artery], below the diagonal artery. The exact location was very fortunate, in that a smaller portion of my heart would be affected."[22]

Clearly, diagnostic tests help doctors pinpoint specific heart problems. This is beneficial because many different things can go wrong in the heart, causing many different symptoms. But with the help of diagnostic tests, problems can be identified and addressed in time to save lives.

Chapter 3

Conventional and Alternative Treatments

Once heart disease has been diagnosed, treatment begins. A number of medications may be prescribed. Because of possible health risks associated with these medications, some people turn to alternative treatments. But when heart disease is life threatening, neither conventional drugs nor alternative treatments may be enough. In these cases, surgery is necessary. No matter what form of treatment is administered, the goal is to keep the heart pumping effectively. How this goal is met depends on the severity and urgency of the problem.

Urgent Treatment for a Heart Attack

Since heart tissue can survive only a few hours after its blood supply has ceased, heart attack victims clearly require immediate treatment. The primary objective is to restore blood flow to the heart, relieve pain, and control arrhythmias. Such treatment usually begins in a hospital emergency room, where medical professionals perform a large number of specialized procedures on the heart attack patient.

Oxygen is administered through an oxygen mask. This helps the patient breathe more easily and increases the supply of oxygenated blood to the heart. At the same time, the patient is given a number of different medications intravenously. These include thrombolytic drugs, which break up blood clots that may be blocking the coronary arteries. Once the blood clots have been dissolved, blood flow through the affected artery is restored. Additionally, anticoagulants may be given to thin the blood, making it easier for the blood to pass through narrowed arteries. Painkilling medicines are also administered.

If a dangerous arrhythmia is detected, the patient may be given an electric shock with an instrument known as a defibrillator. This involves placing two wide paddles over the heart. The paddles are connected to a machine that delivers short, strong electrical jolts to the heart. These jolts help restore the heart's natural rhythm, and if cardiac arrest is occurring, they may stimulate the heart to start beating again.

Once the patient is stabilized and blood flow has been restored to the heart, the patient is placed in a special section of the hospital called the cardiac care unit, or CCU. The CCU has a specially trained

Because the condition of heart attack patients must be closely monitored, they are placed in the hospital's cardiac care unit, where specially trained staff care for them.

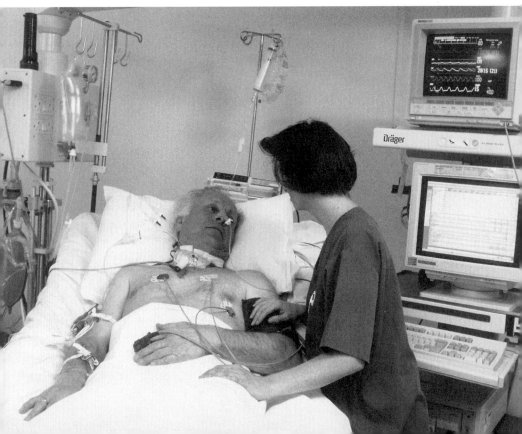

staff and special equipment designed to monitor heart attack patients. Here patients are connected to a heart-monitoring machine similar to an electrocardiogram. This machine is attached to a monitor in the patient's room and another monitor at the nurses' station. It records the patient's blood pressure and heart rhythm so that if a second heart attack should occur, a nurse knows immediately.

The American Heart Association describes the experience of a heart attack patient named Carsten: "Carsten was moved, prodded, poked, and pushed. Somebody gave him oxygen, and someone else started an IV. . . . There was so much going on, it was hard to follow—so much equipment and so many people. . . . Someone said, 'Don't worry, we're going to take care of you.' That was comforting."[23]

Medication

In addition to the medication that is administered while a heart attack is in progress, other medication is commonly prescribed on a long-term basis to treat problems in the heart. Nitroglycerine, for example, is frequently used to treat angina. It is a vasodilator, a drug that causes blood vessels to relax or dilate. Since this facilitates blood flow to the heart, the heart's job is made easier and angina pain is eliminated. But despite its benefits, nitroglycerine can cause side effects, including low blood pressure and severe headaches.

Drugs called beta-blockers are prescribed to reduce the heart's workload. Used to treat angina, heart failure, rapid arrhythmias, and high blood pressure, beta-blockers work by blocking cells known as beta-receptor cells. When the body is under stress, messages from the nervous system stimulate beta-receptor cells to trigger the heart to pump faster and blood vessels to narrow. Beta-blockers attach to these cells, blocking these messages from reaching the heart. Consequently, the heartbeat slows and the heart and blood vessels relax. Blood pressure, angina, and rapid heartbeat are all reduced. Unfortunately, beta-blockers can cause problems. They can cause a patient's blood pressure to drop too low, and the heart to beat dangerously slowly. This can lead to drowsiness, fatigue, dizziness, and fainting.

Statins are another commonly prescribed medication. Statins are cholesterol-lowering drugs that are used to treat atherosclerosis. Statins work by blocking the production of chemicals that are used by the body to manufacture cholesterol, which helps lower a person's overall cholesterol level. This helps slow down the buildup of plaque in the coronary arteries. Marilyn explains how a statin called Lipitor helped her: "Before I started taking Lipitor, my cholesterol was over 300. Since I've been on Lipitor my cholesterol is 155, not great but much better."[24]

Like nitroglycerine and beta-blockers, statins have side effects. Since statins target the liver, where cholesterol is produced, they can cause abnormal liver functions and even lead to liver failure.

Alternative Treatment

In order to avoid the negative side effects of heart medications, many people with heart disease turn to alternative treatments. An alternative treatment is a type of treatment that is not accepted by traditional medical professionals in the United States. Most alternative treatments have not undergone conclusive studies to prove their safety and effectiveness. Therefore, the Food and Drug Administration, whose job it is to verify that the advantages of a treatment exceed any possible health risks as well as to regulate and set standards of use for a treatment, has not approved most alternative treatments for use.

In spite of this, a large number of people have found alternative treatments to be effective in treating heart disease. Many medical professionals agree, especially when conventional treatments are combined with alternative treatments in a method known as complementary treatment. Experts who have used this combination, such as Seth Baum and New York City cardiologist and surgeon Mehmet Oz, say it can reduce cholesterol and alleviate problems resulting from heart failure. As a result, patients need less medication. Mehmet Oz explains: "The revolutionary comingling of conventional medical science and age-old remedies, of West and East [alternative treatment], offers more complete and often more humane treatment than either healing approach by itself. My patients proved this to me."[25]

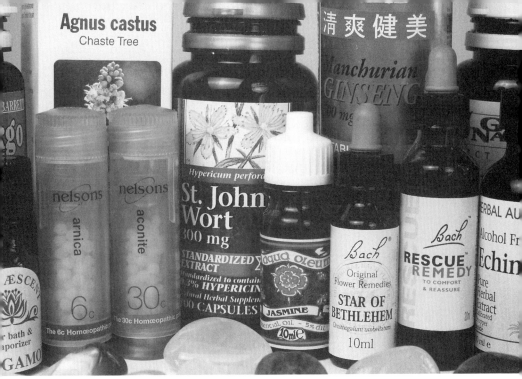

Some people find herbal remedies beneficial to treating heart disease. Doctors caution, however, that herbs are not subject to the same regulations as conventional drugs.

Herbal Treatment

Herbal treatment is one of the most popular forms of alternative treatment for heart disease. Herbal treatment uses the roots, stems, bark, and leaves of plants that are believed to have medicinal value to treat a wide range of illnesses. Ginkgo biloba and ginseng are popular herbs used to treat heart disease. Both contain substances that thin the blood and reduce the stickiness of platelets. This helps keep blood flowing through narrowed arteries and inhibits the buildup of platelets on plaque deposits.

Hawthorn, too, is used to treat heart disease. Hawthorn contains bioflavonoids, plant-based compounds that herbalists say dilate the blood vessels. This helps increase blood flow to the heart. In addition, hawthorn appears to increase the heart's ability to contract, allowing the hearts of people with congestive heart failure to work more efficiently. That is why Seth Baum uses hawthorn to treat his patients. "Among the scores of herbs promoting cardiovascular health, I choose hawthorn. . . . My patients have responded favorably to this herb," the doctor explains.[26]

Although herbs can be beneficial, herbal treatments can pose health risks. Because herbs are natural, many people believe they are safe. However, many herbs are as strong as drugs, and because of the lack of set standards and regulations, some herbal products may be contaminated or stronger than reported on their labels. This can cause a bad reaction. For example, in large doses, ginkgo biloba has been known to cause excessive bleeding that can be potentially life threatening if it is not controlled. Similarly, hawthorn can cause severe headaches and dangerously rapid arrhythmias.

But perhaps the greatest danger arises when people use alternative treatment as a way to avoid surgery, which can be fatal. This is because alternative treatments cannot repair life-threatening arrhythmias. Nor can they restore blood flow to the heart or replace a failing heart. For that matter, neither can conventional drug treatment. In these cases more drastic measures in the form of surgery are needed.

Surgical Treatments

Heart surgery may be fairly simple, such as the implantation of a pacemaker to control a persistent arrhythmia, or quite complex, like bypass surgery. Implantation of a pacemaker involves the insertion of a battery-powered generator about the size of a deck of playing cards under a flap of skin in a person's chest. To do this, the doctor makes a small incision in the chest, creating a pocket. The pacemaker is placed in the pocket and connected to tiny wires that are implanted into the patient's heart. The pacemaker produces electrical impulses that are timed to match the patient's heartbeat. The impulses travel through the wires to the patient's heart, where they stimulate the heart to contract at a steady pace, thus correcting a dangerous arrhythmia.

Most pacemakers last about ten years before the batteries slow down, so doctors must routinely check patients' pacemakers with a special analyzer that detects when a battery is running low. Deborah, who suffers from an arrhythmia caused by congenital heart disease, describes her experience: "I developed a new problem with my heart. I started to have abnormal heart rhythm. . . . Doctors tried to control this with medication, several different kinds, which none worked. . . . The only thing left to do was have a pacemaker put in, as to keep my heart at a normal rate. . . . It is now paced at a normal rate so I don't feel bad anymore."[27]

Angioplasty

Angioplasty is another fairly simple type of heart surgery. It is used to unblock coronary arteries and increase blood flow to the heart. Angioplasty is done under local anesthesia; that is, the patient

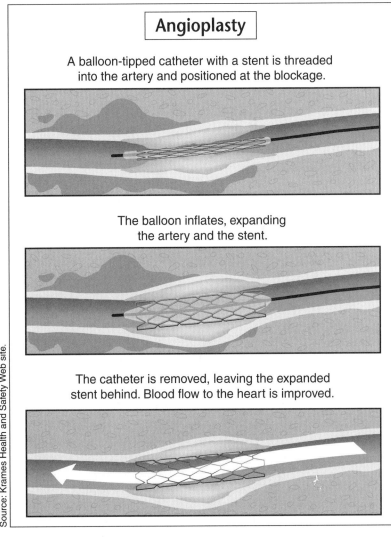

Angioplasty

A balloon-tipped catheter with a stent is threaded into the artery and positioned at the blockage.

The balloon inflates, expanding the artery and the stent.

The catheter is removed, leaving the expanded stent behind. Blood flow to the heart is improved.

Source: Krames Health and Safety Web site.

remains awake during the procedure but feels no pain because the area being operated on is numbed. As in an angiogram, a catheter is threaded through an artery in the groin up to the coronary artery. The catheter has a special balloon tip with a small, expandable mesh tube called a stent. When the catheter reaches the coronary artery, the balloon inflates. This stretches the artery and compresses the plaque against the artery wall, thus improving blood flow to the heart. Once the balloon deflates, the stent, which expanded along with the artery, remains in place to hold the artery open. According to Guidant, a pharmaceutical company that manufactures stents, this procedure eliminates about 90 percent of blockages in coronary arteries.

Perry, who has undergone multiple angioplasties, describes his experience: "For me, angioplasty is a snap. It's slick. They give you something so you can't feel any pain. You can feel the wire being threaded up through you. It feels strange, very strange. I had one stent put in me in 1999. I had another one two years ago. And they're both still working just fine."[28]

Surgeons perform open-heart bypass surgery, a procedure in which a blocked artery is replaced with a piece of vein or artery from another part of the patient's body.

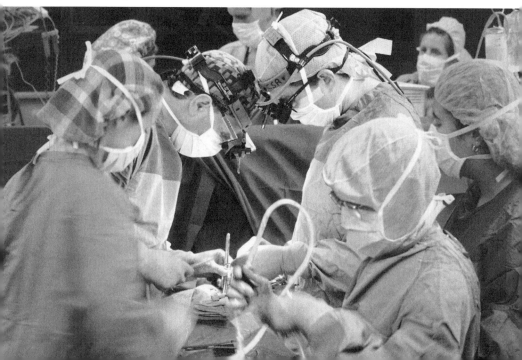

Open-Heart Bypass Surgery

When all the coronary arteries are blocked, or when blockages in a coronary artery are too severe to be helped by angioplasty, open-heart bypass surgery may be necessary. Open-heart bypass surgery is a major surgical procedure that involves the creation of an alternate, or bypass, route around a blocked coronary artery or arteries. In order to do this, the doctor takes a piece of a vein or artery from another part of the body and connects one end to the heart and the other end to a point past the blockage in the coronary artery. As a result, oxygenated blood can flow easily to the heart.

During bypass surgery the patient is sedated. Once the patient is asleep, the surgeon makes a foot-long incision in the patient's chest through the breastbone. Then, in order to have plenty of room to work, the doctor uses a tool called a retractor to pull apart the two halves of the breastbone. Next, the heart is attached to a heart-lung machine, which takes over the heart's pumping action. Otherwise the contraction and relaxation of the heart would make the surgery difficult. It usually takes about an hour for all this to be completed.

Once the machine is doing the heart's job, a drug called a cardioplegic solution is administered through an intravenous tube to stop the heart from functioning. Cardiologist and surgeon Mehmet Oz explains how this affects his patient Richard: "Bright red blood rushes through the pump's tubes into Richard's body, bypassing the heart and returning to the machine as darker oxygen-drained liquid. For the next fifty minutes, Richard's bloodless heart is still."[29]

Before the heart is stopped, the artery or vein that will be used in the bypass is removed from another part of the body. The most common blood vessel used is the saphenous vein, which runs along the inside of the leg. It is used because its job is easily taken over by other veins in the leg once the leg heals. To harvest the vein, an incision is made from the patient's ankle to his or her groin, and the vein is carefully removed. Then this area is sewn up.

Naturally, the vein is cut to the length needed for the bypass. Then one end of the vein is sewn, or grafted, to the heart. The doctor then snips a hole below the blockage in the coronary artery, and the other end of the vein is grafted there. At this point, blood starts flowing around the blockage. Once this happens, the intravenous tube with the cardioplegic solution is removed, as is the heart-lung machine. Then the surgical site is closed up. The breastbone is reconnected with wire, and the incision is sewn or stapled closed.

A Half Million Lives Saved

Bypass surgery usually lasts about three hours. After surgery, the patient is placed in the cardiac care unit of the hospital, where he or she is carefully monitored, and painkillers and anticoagulants are administered. Patients usually stay in the hospital for three to five days, although it takes about six weeks to fully recover.

According to the American Heart Association, about five hundred thousand open-heart bypass surgeries are performed in the United States each year, saving many lives. Seth Baum describes one of his patients:

> His right coronary artery—the only one still functioning at all—had a 95 percent blockage. . . . [The patient] was rushed to an operating room where he underwent multivessel coronary by-pass grafting [heart bypass surgery]. Seven days later, he walked out of the hospital smiling. . . . Without that surgery, his wife would have been a widow and his children fatherless. [30]

Heart Transplant

Not even bypass surgery can save a patient's life when too much heart tissue is damaged and heart failure is occurring. In such a case, a heart transplant may be the only lifesaving treatment available. A heart transplant involves replacing a damaged heart with a healthy heart harvested from a recently deceased person. Hearts are taken from people known as organ donors, who have agreed to donate their vital organs to others upon their deaths. In many states, people who wish to be organ donors sign a permission statement on their driver's license.

Unfortunately, there are more people in need of hearts than there are hearts available. According to the American Heart Association, approximately sixteen thousand Americans would benefit from a heart transplant, but only 2,202 hearts were available in 2001. Because of this, hearts are distributed based on severity of illness.

Complicating matters, hearts must be matched to the recipient's blood type and body weight. Thus, the heart of a child with type A blood would need to be given to another child with type A blood. That child's heart could not be given to a two-hundred-pound man with type B blood.

Consequently, patients are put on a waiting list until a suitable heart is found for them. In the meantime, a left ventricular assist device, or LVAD, may be implanted in the upper part of the patient's abdomen. The LVAD is a battery-operated pumping device that helps the heart pump blood to the rest of the body. It weighs two and a half pounds and is about the size of a portable CD player. A tube connects the LVAD to the patient's heart. The tube pulls blood from the heart to the LVAD, which pumps the blood out to the body. Another tube connects the LVAD to the pump's rechargeable battery, which may be worn on the patient's waist. The pump may be used for up to one year, and without it many people waiting for heart transplants would die. "It's not a question of *would* the patient have died without our help," Oz explains. "He or she would have definitely died. In fact, by federal Food and Drug Administration requirements, before someone gets an LVAD, that person must be clearly close to death."[31]

People with LVADs do not have to live in the hospital, but while they are waiting for a heart, they must carry a pager with them at all times and must never be more than two hours away from the hospital. This is because once a heart is found, time is of the essence. A donated heart can be disconnected from the donor's circulatory system and put in a cold solution, but it will survive for only about four hours. Dawn, the mother of a heart transplant patient, explains: "We were at the circus, when a quiet, suspenseful moment came. We both heard the pager go off, the pager that told us a heart was available. I have never run so fast in my life! We made it to the hospital in record time."[32]

Once a heart is found, the transplant team is assembled. A large number of medical professionals are involved, including one or more transplant surgeons, a cardiologist, an anesthesiologist, and nurses who are specially trained in heart transplant surgery. As soon as the patient arrives at the hospital, the team goes into action. Nurses

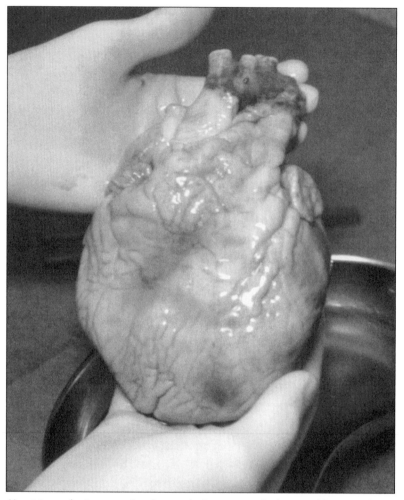

Heart transplant surgery involves replacing a severely damaged heart with a healthy heart harvested from a recently deceased organ donor.

quickly prepare the patient for surgery. First, if necessary, the patient's chest is shaved. Then the patient's chest is washed and painted with a bright yellow or orange antibacterial solution. Next, anesthesia is administered. Once the patient is asleep, a catheter is inserted into a vein in the patient's neck and passed into a coronary artery. This catheter is used to monitor pressure in the patient's heart and oxygen levels in the patient's blood. At the same time, a breathing tube is inserted into the patient's windpipe.

At this point, the surgery begins. In many ways, heart transplant surgery is similar to bypass surgery. The chest is cut and held open in the same way in both procedures, and a heart-lung machine is used. But during heart transplant surgery, most of the patient's heart is removed. The upper back half of the patient's heart, however, is left in place. It acts as support for the new heart and helps the doctor to determine the new heart's exact positioning. The new heart is rested upon the patient's remaining heart muscle and sewn down. Next, the new heart's main arteries are carefully aligned with the patient's coronary arteries and other blood vessels before they are attached. Then the arteries are sewn together. At this point, blood begins to flow over the new heart. The warmth of the blood flowing over the heart usually stimulates it to start beating. If this does not happen, a defibrillator is used. The doctor then checks to make sure there are no leaks where the new heart has been attached. When the doctor is assured that the new heart is working normally, the heart-lung machine is removed and the chest incision is sewn closed.

Transplant surgery usually takes about nine hours. Afterward, patients are kept in the coronary care unit for about ten days. During this time heart transplant patients are administered immunosuppressant drugs that keep the patient's immune system from rejecting the new heart. Transplant patients must take these drugs as long as they live, which may be a long time. In fact, 50 percent of heart transplant patients live at least nine years after their surgery.

Indeed, with the wide range of treatment options available for people with heart disease, most heart disease patients are able to live normal, active lives. David explains:

> Here I am . . . thirty-four years after developing angina, with a body that is a walking testimony to modern medical procedures and devices: five grafts to by-pass my blocked coronary arteries, . . . a pacemaker that beats my heart for me, . . . and three stents to widen my narrowed coronary arteries. Without all this technology, I would have died long ago.[33]

Chapter 4

Living with Heart Disease

L iving with heart disease presents many challenges. Heart attack survivors and people who undergo heart surgery face a two- to three-month recuperation period once they leave the hospital. When this is over, they still face the risk of a heart attack occurring at any time. This causes stress and anxiety. In order to reduce this risk, many people with heart disease make a number of changes in their lives that help them limit further damage to their hearts. In so doing, people with heart disease improve their overall health and the quality of their lives.

Recuperating at Home

One of the first challenges people with heart disease face is recuperating at home after a heart attack or heart surgery. This takes about six weeks, during which patients are unable to return to work or school. Since damaged heart muscle is weak until scar tissue forms, patients are easily fatigued during this recovery period. In fact, it is not uncommon for patients to sleep ten or more hours a night and take frequent naps during the day. Heart attack survivors need extra sleep for about a year following their heart attack. When they are awake, performing even everyday tasks such as cooking or cleaning can be overwhelming. Carlos, a heart attack survivor, explains: "Coming home was a setback. . . . I was tired all the time, unbelievably tired. I remember one day my reading lamp burned out and I went to change the bulb. By the time I walked to the garage, found a bulb, got it out of the package, walked back to the den, unscrewed the bulb, and put in the new one, I thought I'd keel over."[34]

People who undergo bypass or transplant surgery face a number of other challenges. It is not uncommon for these individuals to experience pain for about a month, until their incision heals, as well as memory and concentration problems. Although experts are not sure why memory and concentration difficulties occur, some experts speculate that these may be due to tiny air bubbles that pass through the filter in the heart-lung machine during surgery. These bubbles may temporarily interfere with oxygen reaching the brain, causing these complications. Fortunately, these problems usually disappear within six months. However, as a consequence, while these difficulties persist patients are advised not to drive a motor vehicle.

Patients recovering from heart attack or heart surgery are easily fatigued and often take frequent naps throughout the day.

Maintaining a Balance

Friends and family often help people with heart disease meet these early challenges. Some individuals hire a caregiver to help them deal with everyday activities such as shopping, cooking, driving, and housework. As heart disease patients grow stronger, they gradually become more able to look after themselves.

This, too, can present challenges. In the first few months, it is especially important that people with heart disease are aware of what they can do and what they should avoid doing. This is because their heart muscle is still weak and can easily be stressed, leading to a heart attack. For this reason, activities that involve sudden exertion, such as heavy lifting, sprinting, or digging, should be avoided. Even hot baths, which can raise a person's blood pressure, can be dangerous. Instead, individuals are advised to take showers.

Patients must be cautious even when it comes to gentle activities. For example, people with heart disease are encouraged to take short walks to strengthen their heart once they feel able. But they are also warned not to overexert themselves. Gradually and incrementally increasing their activity level helps people with heart disease meet this challenge, as does stopping and resting whenever they feel tired.

Cardiac Rehabilitation

Participating in a cardiac rehabilitation program is another way people with heart disease strengthen their heart while preventing damage. Cardiac rehabilitation programs begin while patients are still in the hospital, where patients and their families are given pamphlets about heart disease and advice about their medication and about handling their recovery at home. Then, after two to three months at home, patients begin attending rehabilitation sessions. These sessions, usually held at a fitness center in a hospital, involve medically supervised group exercise at least three times a week for about six to twelve weeks. These sessions usually include aerobic exercise of gradually increasing difficulty. Walking on a treadmill or riding an exercise bicycle are typical exercises.

The participants are both adults and children with heart disease, with some hospitals offering special sessions for children with con-

After two or three months of recovery, patients typically participate in a cardiac rehabilitation program involving medically supervised group exercise.

genital heart disease. No matter the age of the participants, all sessions are supervised by cardiac nurses. These nurses provide participants with encouragement and support, while carefully monitoring each participant's health. Tami describes her experience: "When you go to cardiac rehab, you're exercising, but you feel safe because you have monitors. You learn to feel what's normal and what's not normal."[35]

Besides exercise, cardiac rehabilitation programs also provide information on living with heart disease. This includes information about different heart problems and their treatments, as well as ways to make lifestyle changes that reduce heart disease risk factors. In addition, participants provide each other with social and psychological support. Verne explains: "From the first moment, I thought it was absolutely terrific. What I liked most were the many friends I made there and the wonderful support group it rapidly became—this included the other participants, of course, but the staff as well."[36]

Attending a cardiac rehabilitation program can help people with heart disease take more control of their lives and lessen their risk of having a heart attack. According to cardiologist and Tufts University professor James M. Rippe, in the three years following a heart attack, heart attack survivors who participate in a cardiac rehabilitation program are 25 percent less likely to die of a heart attack than survivors who do not participate in cardiac rehabilitation.

Dietary Changes

One of the topics patients learn about in cardiac rehabilitation is the importance of eating a heart-healthy diet. For example, the American Heart Association advises people with heart disease, especially those with high blood pressure, to follow a low-salt diet of no more than twenty-four hundred milligrams of salt each day. This is because dietary salt raises blood pressure. Scientists do not know why this is so. Many people with high blood pressure eliminate salty foods such as salted pretzels and chips from their diet, often eating fresh fruit and vegetables instead. They also avoid adding salt to their food, substituting other spices such as garlic to enhance the food's flavor. The American Heart Association describes one woman's efforts to help her husband follow a low-sodium, heart-healthy diet: "Instead of potato chips, Connie set out a bowl of finger-sized carrots, celery sticks, zucchini spears and green onions. . . . She also served salt-free pretzels."[37]

People with heart disease are also advised to limit dietary fat. Since dietary fat is turned into cholesterol by the liver, eating a low-fat diet is an important step toward reducing atherosclerosis and protecting the heart. In fact, according to a 2002 study at Osaka City University in Japan, even one high-fat meal can lead to trouble. In this study, fifteen healthy men were each given a shake containing one hundred grams of fat, about the equivalent of the fat contained in a double cheeseburger and a large order of fries. Then blood flow through their coronary arteries was monitored. After five hours, the subjects' coronary blood flow dropped by 18 percent. When the subjects were fed another shake containing ten grams of fat, their coronary blood flow did not decrease. The researchers concluded that high-fat meals make it harder for blood to reach the heart, and may be particularly harmful for people with atherosclerosis who already have circulatory problems.

Of all fats, foods rich in saturated fats, such as beef, lamb, pork, butter, milk, ice cream, and cheese, appear to raise LDL levels the most. So, too, do foods high in a man-made fat known as trans fat, which is found in many fried and processed foods as well as cookies, crackers, chips, and margarine. In order to protect the heart, the American Heart Association suggests limiting daily fat intake to no more than 30 percent of total daily caloric intake. Of this, no more than 10 percent should be saturated and trans fat. Therefore, people with heart disease try to eliminate these foods from their diets, substituting fish, chicken, beans, fruit, vegetables, trans fat–free magarine, and low-fat milk and cheese for fatty foods. These products contain less saturated and trans fat and are thus healthier for the heart. Steve, a heart attack survivor, describes the changes he made:

> Of course I changed my diet. I use to eat two fried eggs with sausage for breakfast, and pizza for lunch every day. The big thing I had trouble with was cheese. I like cheese, and that's a cholesterol bomb. Now I eat much less cheese, less red meat, less processed food, less fried food, and more fish.[38]

Losing Weight

Making dietary changes is especially important for overweight individuals who have heart disease because excess weight strains the heart. Moreover, overweight people usually eat more dietary fat than they need, which raises blood cholesterol levels. Being overweight is also linked to heart failure and high blood pressure. According to the American Heart Association, overweight people are three times more likely to have high blood pressure than normal-weight people, and as a person's weight increases, so does his or her blood pressure. Conversely, weight loss decreases blood pressure. Consequently, it is not surprising that, according to James M. Rippe, 75 percent of deaths of obese people are linked to heart disease.

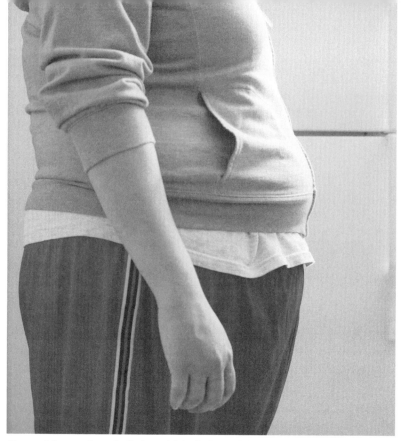

Overweight people typically have high cholesterol levels and high blood pressure, putting them at a substantially higher risk for developing heart disease.

Therefore, it is important that overweight people with heart disease lose weight. In fact, every major medical organization in the United States that deals with heart disease, including the American Heart Association, and the American Medical Association, advocate weight loss for overweight heart disease patients.

Losing weight is difficult for everyone. It can be particularly hard for people with heart disease because the type of diet they may follow is limited. For example, the American Heart Association warns people, especially those with heart disease, to avoid fad diets. Such diets, which help many people lose weight quickly, can be risky for people with heart disease. For example, popular high-protein diets usually are high in fat. Popular appetite suppressant pills can also be risky, since they raise blood pressure. And many fad diets stimulate rapid weight loss, but when dieters go off these diets they often gain the weight back. Such weight fluctuations are particularly risky for people with heart disease. In fact, researchers at the University of Michigan at Ann Arbor found in 2003 that subjects whose weight fluctuates have weaker hearts and poorer blood flow to the heart than those who lose weight slowly and maintain their new weight.

Instead of fad diets, the American Heart Association advises overweight people with heart disease to switch to a heart-healthy,

The American Heart Association produces books and other popular media to promote a healthy lifestyle that reduces the risk of heart disease.

low-fat diet, in which dieters consume fewer calories than they burn. This diet should consist of 15 percent protein, less than 30 percent fat, and 55 percent complex carbohydrates such as cereal, whole-grain bread, fruits, and vegetables.

Breaking Unhealthy Habits

Dietary changes include not only lowering dietary fat and calories, but also avoiding habit-forming substances like caffeine and tobacco. Nicotine in tobacco and caffeine in products such as coffee and colas speed up the heart rate and raise blood pressure. In fact, according to cardiac rehabilitation program psychologist and heart disease expert Wayne M. Sotile, smoking even one cigarette causes people's heart rates to increase by twenty-five beats per minute, and increases their blood pressure by twenty points. While caffeine's effect is not as drastic, it still increases blood pressure by four millimeters and heart rate by two beats per minute, according to an article in the July/August 2003 issue of *Men's Health* magazine.

Moreover, both substances cause blood vessels throughout the body to constrict. This makes it harder for blood to reach the heart. And because caffeine and tobacco are stimulants, they elevate the body's response to stress, which can be dangerous for people with heart disease.

Smoking is so dangerous that heart attack survivors who continue to smoke are three times more likely than heart attack survivors who stop smoking to have another heart attack within a year. What's more, when heart attack survivors who smoke have another heart attack, it is more likely to be fatal than it is for those who have quit. "After my first heart attack," recalls Jerry, "my cardiologist told me to never smoke again, that smoking was the cause of 450,000 premature deaths a year from various causes."[39]

Since nicotine is addictive, it is hard to stop smoking, and some methods that help people quit are inappropriate for people with heart disease. For example, nicotine replacement therapy, which involves chewing nicotine gum or wearing a nicotine patch instead of smoking a cigarette, can be harmful for people who recently had a heart attack as well as those with angina or an arrhythmia. This is because even small doses of nicotine can worsen these problems.

Doctors encourage patients suffering from heart disease to exercise regularly. Light to moderate exercise such as walking helps to maintain healthy weight and reduces stress.

Many cardiac rehabilitation programs offer special counseling sessions aimed at helping participants to stop smoking. Many people with heart disease quit smoking "cold turkey." This means they stop all at once. Many of these people become smoke-free while they are in the hospital, where smoking is forbidden. Steve explains: "If I hadn't gone to the hospital, I would probably have never quit smoking. No cigarettes for my hospital stay, and that's how I busted it. It's been three years now, and I haven't had a cigarette since."[40]

Following an Exercise Program

Leading a sedentary lifestyle is another unhealthy habit that people with heart disease are advised to change. Once cardiac rehabilitation is over, people with heart disease are told to continue exercising on their own. Exercise is important to keeping the heart healthy. Not only does it make the heart stronger, it helps people with heart disease maintain a healthy weight and reduces stress and anxiety.

Any form of exercise can reduce stress and strengthen the heart. People with heart disease, however, must be careful not to overtax their hearts. For instance, people with angina are advised to keep their exercise level below the point at which they experience chest pain. People with high blood pressure, too, must be careful. Strength training such as weight lifting can cause rapid spikes in blood pressure. In addition, lifting heavy weights can cause weak heart tissue to tear.

People with heart failure and children with certain types of heart defects also face special challenges when exercising. These individuals are encouraged to exercise in order to increase the efficiency of their hearts, but at the same time they must be careful not to overstress their hearts, since their hearts do not pump sufficient blood. Therefore, the American Heart Association recommends that people with heart disease perform light to moderate exercise, depending on the condition of their heart and coronary arteries. People exercising at a suitable level should be able to talk while they are exercising; if they are too winded to talk, they are overexerting themselves.

Optimally, people with heart disease should practice some form of exercise for twenty to thirty minutes a day, at least three times a week. Walking, biking, swimming, yoga, golfing, and dancing are just a few of the exercises that people with heart disease enjoy. Brad Henson, a heart attack survivor and author, started a walking program after recovering from a heart attack. He explains: "The added

First Lady Laura Bush is the keynote speaker at a conference hosted by a support group for women with heart disease. Many such support groups exist in the United States.

benefit of my walking program was that my heart muscle was getting stronger and stronger. My doctor explained to me that a well-conditioned heart muscle becomes more powerful. . . . Because I was exercising the heart muscle, it became better at pumping blood throughout the body."[41]

Reducing Stress

Reducing stress is another lifestyle change people with heart disease are urged to make. Like exercise, meditation is a way people with heart disease reduce stress. Meditation entails freeing the mind of worrisome thoughts in order to relax the body and relieve stress. In order to do this, meditators use a concentration technique in which they silently repeat a word or phrase, called a mantra, until their minds are quiet and all stressful thoughts are gone. People who meditate report feeling extremely relaxed after as little as twenty minutes of meditation. Indeed, in 2003, researchers at Thomas Jefferson University in Philadelphia, Pennsylvania, found that daily meditation reduces feelings of stress by 25 percent. This is especially important for people with heart disease who, according to researchers at the University of Florida in Gainesville, are three times more likely to die from a heart-related problem when they are under stress than when they are not.

Getting Support

Another way people with heart disease deal with stress, as well as other emotional issues such as anxiety and fear, is by joining a support group. Many individuals find support among their peers in cardiac rehabilitation. Once the program ends, they often find that joining a formal support group helps them cope with the challenges they face. Heart disease support groups are sponsored by organizations such as the American Heart Association. Meetings for people of all ages are held all over the country, as well as online. There are even special groups for young people with congenital heart defects and for their parents.

In heart disease support groups, individuals with heart disease share their feelings and experiences, as well as information and encouragement. "Being part of a support group provides its members with a feeling that they are not alone in the universe, and that there is someone else that has walked in their shoes, and can fully understand what they are going through,"[42] Brad Henson explains.

Young people with congenital heart disease can find additional support by attending medically supervised summer camps just for children with congenital heart disease. Run by groups such as the American Heart Association, these camps allow young heart disease patients to have fun participating in activities such as swimming, crafts, horseback riding, and games in a medically supervised environment. Here, health-care professionals plan activities that will not tax campers' hearts and also monitor campers' health and safety. There are also educational programs in which these youth learn more about heart disease and ways to cope with the challenges they face. Moreover, attending these camps allows children with heart disease to connect with and gain the support of other children with similar health challenges.

Long-Term Medical Monitoring

Joining a support group, making dietary changes, and breaking unhealthy habits do help protect people's hearts. But in order to ensure that their hearts are functioning properly, people with heart disease must have medical checkups every six months. During these checkups, patients are examined, their blood pressure and pulse are measured, and an EKG and a blood cholesterol test are administered. This helps the doctor to ascertain whether the patient's medication is working properly, and to detect and treat any problems before they can worsen. Perry explains, "I go back to the doctor for checkups every six months. I have a blood test and an EKG. The last visit, the doctor said everything was just fine. If not, the doctor gets me fixed right up."[43]

It is clear that living with heart disease presents many challenges. But by adopting a healthy lifestyle, people with heart disease can live long, healthy lives. Heart attack survivor Gerry is one example. An article on the American Heart Association's Web site quotes Gerry and talks about his lifestyle changes: "Gerry is . . . continuing to eat healthy foods and gets lots of exercise to do his best to prevent another heart attack. . . . 'I think I'm in better shape now than before,' he says. 'I'm in my golden years and they're the best years of my life.'"[44]

Chapter 5

What the Future Holds

In an effort to prevent coronary heart disease, scientists are investigating its causes. Scientists know that when plaque or a blood clot blocks a coronary artery, the result is coronary heart disease. However, they theorize that this may not be the only contributing factor. Therefore, researchers are investigating other factors that may play a role in causing heart disease. Once they identify the causes of heart disease, they hope to develop therapies that address each factor and thus stop coronary heart disease before it begins. At the same time, scientists are working on creating new and more effective treatments to help patients who already have heart disease.

Blood Factors

Since coronary heart disease is a disease of the circulatory system, scientists are examining and comparing blood samples of people with and without coronary heart disease. They already know that the blood of people with coronary heart disease usually contains elevated levels of LDLs, while that of healthy people does not. They are examining other components of blood from both groups in an effort to determine whether the blood of people with coronary heart disease contains inappropriate levels of other blood factors. Once these features can be identified, scientists can develop treatments to regulate them.

C-reactive Protein and Inflammation

One common blood property scientists have found in people with coronary heart disease is an elevated level of C-reactive protein,

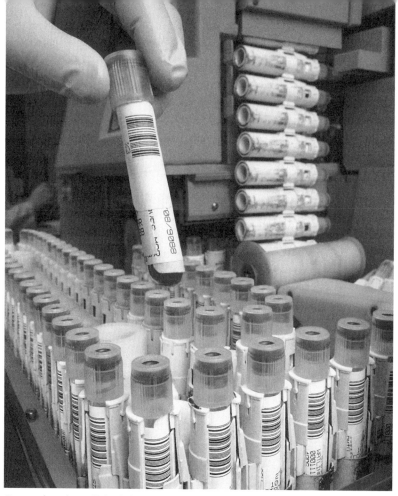

Researchers have linked the elevated levels of certain substances found in blood samples taken from heart disease patients with the onset of the disease.

or CRP. CRP is produced by the body in response to inflammation and CRP levels increase whenever there is inflammation anywhere in the body.

Inflammation, which causes swelling, redness, and heat, is the body's way of responding to infection and injury. Scientists do not know what causes CRP levels to rise in people with coronary heart disease. They theorize that a persistent infection in the heart or coronary arteries may cause inflammation in the blood vessels. This hastens the buildup of plaque and the formation of danger-ous blood clots.

In 2003 scientists at the National Public Health Institute in Oulu, Finland, concluded an eight-year study to investigate this theory. The study analyzed the blood of 241 heart attack victims and 241 healthy subjects for the presence of CRP and *C. pneumoniae,* a bacterium that causes pneumonia. The scientists found *C. pneumoniae* and elevated levels of CRP in the blood of the heart attack victims. Moreover, the subjects with chronically elevated levels of *C. pnuemoniae* and CRP were four times more likely to suffer from a heart attack than those subjects with normal levels of these blood factors.

Scientists have not yet determined whether the presence of *C. pnuemoniae* or any other bacterium or virus is definitely a factor in causing heart disease, but other studies are planned. If scientists prove that a virus or bacterium is a factor in heart disease, antibiotics or antiviral medicines may someday be used to prevent heart attacks. In the meantime, the American Heart Association suggests that a blood test for CRP be administered to people at risk of heart disease. Cardiologist Paul Ridker of Harvard University Medical School explains: "With a large segment of the population at moderate risk, [CRP tests] will help them to know what their true risk is."[45]

If blood tests indicate elevated CRP levels, people can then take steps to lower their risk of heart attack. In fact, many health-care professionals advise people with elevated CRP to take an aspirin every day. This is because aspirin has anti-inflammatory properties that counter the effect of inflammation and the dangerous blood clots that can result.

Homocysteine and Fibrinogen

Scientists have also linked elevated levels of homocysteine, an amino acid found in everyone's blood, and fibrinogen, a chemical that promotes blood clots, with coronary heart disease. In 2000 Massachusetts scientists involved in the Framingham Heart Study checked fibrinogen levels in the blood of 2,632 subjects. They found that fibrinogen levels were highest in the subjects with heart disease. Since fibrinogen is another indicator of inflammation, scientists theorize that inflammation in the coronary arteries elevates fibrinogen production. Elevated fibrinogen causes the blood to clot, which can lead to heart attacks.

A homocysteine is an amino acid that is produced in the body during the digestion of meat. Like cholesterol, homocysteine helps the body build healthy tissue and is also linked to the formation of plaque. Normally, excess homocysteine is eliminated from the body in urine. Therefore, healthy people rarely have elevated levels of homocysteine in their bloodstream. However, studies from as far back as 1968 have found elevated homocysteine levels in people with heart disease. For example, a 1992 Harvard University study tracked fifteen thousand people for five years. The study found that people with the highest homocysteine levels were three times more likely to have a heart attack than those with lower levels. Scientists do not know why homocysteine levels are elevated in people with heart disease, but speculate that for unknown reasons these people's bodies are unable to eliminate the substance.

Although scientists have not yet definitively proven that elevated fibrinogen and homocysteine levels are factors in causing heart disease, studies are ongoing. Moreover, many physicians test for these substances in the blood of patients at risk of heart disease. If an elevated level of either substance is found, doctors may more closely monitor the patient or prescribe more aggressive treatment such as statin drugs, which appear to lower homocysteine levels and inhibit blood clots. Cardiologist Geoffrey H. Tofler of Royal North Shore Hospital in Sydney, Australia, explains: "If I'm uncertain about what level of therapy a patient requires—whether someone should be given a cholesterol-lowering drug, for example—finding high fibrinogen would tend to make me take a more aggressive approach in treatment. Conversely, finding low or normal fibrinogen would reassure me."[46]

Diet and Blood Factors

Interestingly, while investigating the role that blood factors play in coronary heart disease, scientists found that homocysteine and fibrinogen levels are commonly elevated in Americans and western Europeans. Both are groups with a high incidence of coronary heart disease. Conversely, levels of these blood factors and LDL levels are usually low among the Japanese, natives of the Greek island of Crete, and Greenland Eskimos, while their HDL levels are high. Not surprisingly, the Japanese, Cretans, and Greenlanders have the lowest incidence of heart disease in the world. Since dietary factors encourage the development of elevated LDLs,

Greenland Eskimos like these women rarely develop heart disease. Scientists attribute this fact to the large amount of fish in their diets.

scientists are examining the diets of these three groups in hopes of identifying a dietary factor that may somehow discourage the development of heart disease.

One factor scientists have pinpointed is that people in each of these groups eats fish an average of at least five times a week. Fish is rich in an essential nutrient known as omega-3 fatty acid, which scientists speculate inhibits the development of heart disease. Scientists think that, like all fat, omega-3 fatty acid is converted to cholesterol by the liver. But for unknown reasons, omega-3 fatty acid attaches to HDLs rather than LDLs. This helps eliminate plaque-forming LDLs from the body.

In addition, omega-3 fatty acid contains two substances, eicosapentaenoic acid (EPA) and docosahexaenoic acid (DHA), which scientists think reduce the stickiness of platelets, thus hindering the development of plaque deposits and blood clots. These two substances also appear to slow down and even prevent rapid arrhythmias, although scientists do not know why.

Researchers began examining the effects of omega-3 fatty acid on the heart in the 1980s when they noticed that the diet of Greenland Eskimos, a group in which heart disease is almost nonexistent, is 70 percent fish. Since then, a number of studies have been conducted. One 2002 Harvard School of Public Health study conducted in Boston investigated the link between omega-3 fatty acid and heart disease prevention by examining the diet of eighty-five thousand women for a sixteen-year period. The study found that women who ate fish five times a week were 34 percent less likely than those who rarely ate fish to develop heart disease. Moreover, the frequent fish eaters were 45 percent less likely to die from heart-related problems. Other studies have had similar results. For instance, a Finnish study reported in the November 28, 2000, issue

Studies indicate that the omega-3 fatty acid commonly found in fish helps reduce artery plaque deposits and blood clots.

of the American Heart Association journal *Circulation* examined the amount of DHA in the blood of 1,871 men. The study found that the men with the highest levels of DHA were 44 percent less likely to have a heart attack than were those men with the lowest levels.

As a result of these and other studies, the American Heart Association recommends that people eat fish at least twice a week. Also, many people with heart disease take omega-3 fatty acid dietary supplements. Once researchers have proven conclusively that a deficiency of omega-3 fatty acid promotes heart disease, such supplements may commonly be prescribed for everyone. But since omega-3 fatty acid affects the blood's ability to clot and can lead to dangerous bleeding, more research must be done.

The Role of Vitamins

In looking at the diets of Greenland Eskimos, the Japanese, and the people of Crete, another factor scientists have pinpointed is that the Japanese and Cretans consume large quantities of fresh fruit, vegetables, and legumes. The typical Western diet is often low in these nutrients.

Fruits, vegetables, and legumes contain a wide variety of vitamins and minerals, including vitamins A, C, and E, all of which are antioxidants. This means they contain chemicals that prevent oxidation, a process in which cells are changed or damaged by contact with oxygen molecules in the bloodstream. Some scientists theorize that oxidation causes LDLs to become sticky, and thus harmful. Adequate consumption of antioxidants, they say, prevents this from happening.

Therefore, many scientists think that a deficiency in antioxidants leads to coronary heart disease. A 1993 study at Harvard University tested this theory. A group of nurses were each given four hundred milligrams of a vitamin E supplement every day for two years, while a control group was given a placebo. The group that took vitamin E was 46 percent less likely than the control group to suffer from coronary heart disease.

Although scientists have not yet proven that dietary deficiencies can cause heart disease, many people are taking steps to add more fish, fruit, vegetables, and legumes to their diets. Moreover, doctors are advising patients with heart disease to take a daily vitamin supplement, and many people without heart disease are doing just that in an effort to prevent it. Heart attack survivor Brad Henson explains: "My belief is that my heart attack could have been completely avoided, if I would have known the information . . . about vitamins, minerals, and trace minerals."[47]

Genetics

As some scientists focus their attention on dietary and blood factors, other scientists are examining the role genetics plays in causing heart disease. In fact, in 2003, scientists at the Cleveland Clinic in Ohio identified a mutant gene they say is linked to heart attacks. The scientists examined the genes of one hundred members of a family in which multiple generations suffer from heart disease. The scientists found that all the members of the family who had a mutated form of a gene known as MEF2A suffered from, or later developed, heart disease, while those without the mutated gene remained healthy. In its normal state, the gene inhibits the growth and buildup of plaque in the coronary arteries. The scientists theorize that this protection does not exist in people with the mutated gene. As a consequence, plaque growth and coronary artery blockages are accelerated, and heart attacks are almost inevitable. Researcher Eric J. Topol says of the family's MEF2A gene, "This is the first heart attack gene. Everyone who has this gene mutation is destined to have the disease. If you don't have this gene in this family, you appear to be free from developing the disease."[48]

Scientists are currently investigating whether all people with heart disease carry the mutated gene, or if its presence is limited to the family studied. If it is found in all people with heart disease, scientists hope to develop a substance to alter the gene. Until such a substance is developed, testing of the gene mutation combined with statin medication for healthy patients with the mutated gene is likely to become routine.

Developing New Treatments

While some scientists are investigating possible causes of heart disease, others are creating new, more effective treatments. One treat-

Scientists are researching the role that genetics plays in the development of heart disease by studying families in which multiple generations suffer from the disease.

ment being perfected by scientists at the University of London in England utilizes what scientists have learned about the link between nutritional deficiencies and heart disease to make a new pill aimed at preventing heart attacks. The pill, known as the polypill, combines folic acid, a B vitamin found in vegetables and legumes, with three blood pressure–lowering medications and a statin drug, a beta-blocker, and aspirin. The pill's objective is to lower cholesterol, blood pressure, homocysteine levels, and platelet stickiness.

Scientists estimate that the pill will cause negative side effects in 8 to 15 percent of the people treated with it. However, it also will reduce heart attacks by 88 percent, and add about eleven years of life free from heart disease to one-third of all people over age fifty-five who take it. According to the *British Medical Journal,* "The polypill strategy would largely prevent heart attacks and strokes if taken by everyone age 55 and older and everyone with existing cardiovascular disease. It would be acceptably safe and with widespread use would have a greater impact on prevention of disease in the Western world than any other single intervention."[49]

Since the polypill would treat all people age fifty-five and over, including those with no risk factors or signs of heart disease, it is considered by some physicians to be a radical treatment. Therefore, more study into its effectiveness is being conducted. Many scientists say it may become a widespread heart disease–prevention therapy in the near future.

Synthetic Cholesterol

Another newly developed drug is a laboratory-produced version of a highly effective type of high-density lipoprotein. In a 2003 study at the Cleveland Clinic, the drug was administered intravenously once a week for five weeks to thirty-six patients who had had heart attacks or angina. At the same time, eleven patients received a placebo. After six weeks all the patients received echocardiograms, which showed a 4 percent reduction in plaque buildup in the patients who received the drug treatment, but no change in the placebo group. The drug clears excess cholesterol from the coronary arteries and then is eliminated from the body. "The concept is a sort of liquid Drano for the coronary arteries,"[50] study director and cardiologist Steven Nissan explains.

The test result is especially encouraging because it yielded this reduction in plaque deposits in so brief a time. For example, statin drugs typically reduce cholesterol by 3 percent after being taken for at least six months. Scientists theorize that if this new treatment is extended over a longer period, it might completely clear all plaque deposits from the body. A number of long-term studies are being planned, as well as studies in which an attempt will be made to convert the medication from intravenous form into pill form. Scientists all over the United States are optimistic about the results. Jonathan Abrams, professor of medicine and cardiology chief at the University of New Mexico Hospital, explains: "It's very big, exciting news. It provides an entirely new approach to treating heart disease, although it's certainly not ready for prime time."[51]

A Vaccine to Regulate Cholesterol

Scientists at Avant Immunotherapeutics, a pharmaceutical company in Needham, Massachusetts, are taking another approach. They are developing a vaccine that reduces the production of LDLs

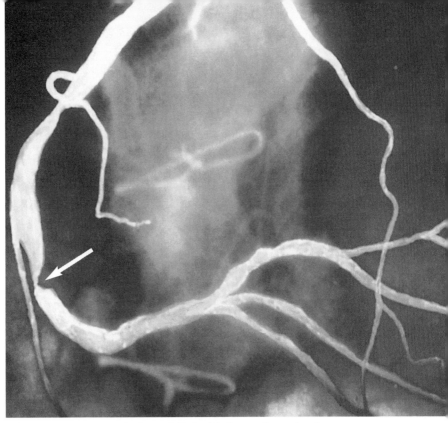

A blocked artery is visible (lower left) in this X-ray of a patient's coronary arteries. Researchers are developing new drugs that reduce the plaque responsible for such blockages.

while increasing the production of HDLs. The vaccine contains a protein that stops cholesterol from attaching to LDLs and stimulates cholesterol to attach to HDLs. This causes the body to produce more HDLs to carry the cholesterol.

The vaccine, which must be administered twice a year, is predicted to raise HDL levels by 50 percent. Indeed, in animal tests in which rabbits were placed on a high-fat diet and administered the vaccine, HDL levels increased by 42 percent and LDL levels decreased by 24 percent. Moreover, plaque deposits were reduced by 40 percent. Based on the results of the animal study, clinical trials in which the vaccine is being tested on humans are currently under way. So far, the results have been encouraging. According to Ronald Krauss of the American Heart Association, "It's a very new approach that has a lot of potential."[52] Before the vaccine can be approved for general use, however, scientists must determine the safest and most effective dosage.

Improving Heart Surgery

At the same time that some scientists are developing new medications, others are devising methods to make heart surgery easier and less invasive. Robotic surgery, which is being tested as a
substitute for open-heart bypass surgery, is one such method. During robotic surgery, a surgeon sits in front of a computer monitor
that gives him or her a magnified three-dimensional view of the
patient, as well as all the surgical tools needed for heart surgery.
The tools are attached to movable robotic arms. As if playing a
video game, the surgeon manipulates controls similar to joysticks
that move the arms in order to perform surgery.

Robotic heart surgery has many advantages over traditional bypass surgery. First, the robotic arms are more flexible and can turn
and bend better than human hands. This allows the surgeon to get
to areas that might otherwise be unreachable. Moreover, the arms

*A surgeon controls robotic arms during a coronary artery bypass. Robotic surgery
is much safer than traditional surgery and requires shorter recovery time.*

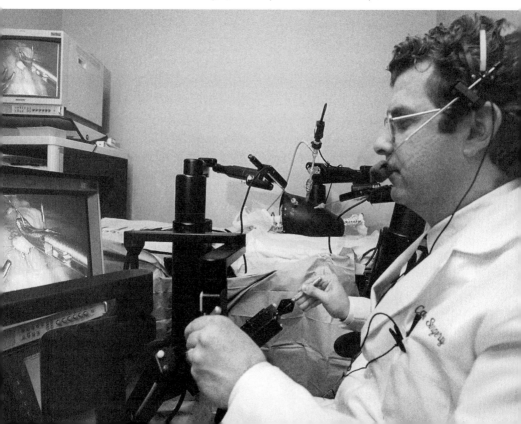

are always steady, unlike human fingers, which may tremble, causing dangerous mistakes. Says Sudhir Srivastava, a cardiologist who has tested the use of the robotic arm in five robotic bypass heart surgeries at Odessa Regional Hospital in Texas, "I think the robot probably operates better than the human hand."[53]

Another advantage is that during robotic surgery the patient's chest is better magnified than in traditional surgery. In addition, the doctor can adjust lenses to zoom in and out of the operating field. This allows the surgeon to view areas that might otherwise be difficult or even impossible to see, and if these areas are in need of care, the doctor can then proceed to work on them.

Perhaps the most significant advantage is that the robotic arms can work in a small area. Therefore, it is unnecessary for the doctor to make a foot-long incision in the patient's chest. Instead, an incision of six inches or less is all that is needed. This reduces post-surgery chest pain as well as recovery time. In fact, unlike in traditional open-heart surgery, patients who undergo robotic surgery can usually leave the hospital in one to three days, and return to their normal lives in less than half the usual recovery time. A 2002 *Dallas Morning News* article quotes a patient: "'I feel great. No pain at all,' said Domingo Anaya, who had closed chest robotic bypass surgery by Dr. Srivastava on Nov. 11. He went home the next day, and is already taking short strolls in his neighborhood."[54]

Besides Srivastava's work, robotic heart surgery has been successfully used to repair holes in the hearts of sixteen patients with congenital birth defects, according to a 2002 study at Columbia University College of Physicians and Surgeons in New York City. It is also being used nationwide to repair damaged heart valves and has been approved by the federal government for this use. It has not yet been approved for general use in bypass surgery, however, and is currently being tested to ensure the procedure's safety and effectiveness. Moreover, because each robotic arm costs about $1 million and many surgeons are not yet comfortable performing robotic surgery, it may take time before it replaces traditional open-heart bypass surgery. Despite these problems, many doctors predict that robotic heart surgery will eventually become more common than traditional bypass surgery.

With new heart treatments being developed and new discoveries being made into the disease's possible causes almost every day, the future looks bright for people with heart disease. In fact, the death rate from coronary heart disease has decreased by 25 percent since 1990, and children with congenital heart defects who probably would have died twenty years ago are now living long lives. Moreover, most experts predict things will be even better in the future. Kim Eagle, director of Ann Arbor's University of Michigan Cardiovascular Center, says, "I've never been more optimistic."[55]

Notes

Introduction: The Leading Cause of Death in America

1. Fred Abatemarco, "My Heart Attack," *Men's Health,* September 2002, p. 155.
2. Quoted in Katherine Griffin, "This Healthy Woman Had a Heart Attack. Could You?" *Good Housekeeping,* October 2003, p. 100.
3. Quoted in Samuel M. Fox, *Heart Attack! Advice for Patients by Patients.* New Haven, CT: Yale University Press, 2002, p. 42.

Chapter 1: What Is Heart Disease?

4. Anna Jaworski, "Growing Up with Congenital Heart Defects," Baby Hearts Press. www.babyheartspress.com.
5. Seth Baum, *The Total Guide to a Healthy Heart.* New York: Kensington Books, 1999, p. 15.
6. Dawn Martin, "The Heart of a Mother," Baby Hearts Press. www.babyheartspress.com.
7. Quoted in Fox, *Heart Attack!,* p. 81
8. John, personal interview with the author in Las Cruces, New Mexico, November 1, 2003.
9. Abatemarco, "My Heart Attack," p. 155.
10. Perry, personal interview with the author in Las Cruces, New Mexico, September 29, 2003.
11. John, personal interview with the author.

Chapter 2: Symptoms and Diagnosis

12. Kari Barr, "The Heart of a Mother: Chapter 2, Letting Go," Baby Hearts Press. www.babyheartspress.com.
13. Perry, personal interview with the author.
14. Marilyn, telephone interview with the author, October 29, 2003.

15. Abatemarco, "My Heart Attack," p. 154.
16. Perry, personal interview with the author.
17. Quoted in Fox, *Heart Attack!*, p. 49.
18. Heart Center Online, "Getting My Natural Rhythm Back." www. heartcenteronline.com.
19. Heart Center Online, "My 43 Year Young Heart." www.heartcenter online.com.
20. Community Blood Center, "Donor's Baby Benefits from the Community Blood Center." www.kcblood.org.
21. Marilyn, telephone interview with the author.
22. Quoted in Fox, *Heart Attack!*, p. 30.

Chapter 3: Conventional and Alternative Treatments
23. American Heart Association, *American Heart Association Guide to Heart Attack Treatment, Recovery, and Prevention.* New York: Times Books, 1996, p. 35.
24. Marilyn, telephone interview with the author.
25. Mehmet Oz, *Healing from the Heart: A Leading Heart Surgeon Explores the Power of Complementary Medicine.* New York: Dutton, 1998, p. 9.
26. Baum, *The Total Guide to a Healthy Heart*, p. 202.
27. Deborah L. Dupere, "The Life I Have Lived and Still Live with Heart and Lung Problems," Cardiac Experience Journal, Children's Hospital Boston. www.experiencejournal.com.
28. Perry, personal interview with the author.
29. Oz, *Healing from the Heart*, p. 15.
30. Baum, *The Total Guide to a Healthy Heart*, p. 8.
31. Oz, *Healing from the Heart*, p. 22.
32. Martin, "The Heart of a Mother."
33. Quoted in Fox, *Heart Attack!*, p. 74.

Chapter 4: Living with Heart Disease
34. Quoted in Wayne M. Sotile, *Thriving with Heart Disease: A Unique Program for You and Your Family: Live Happier, Healthier, Longer.* New York: Free Press, 2003, p. 18.
35. Quoted in Susan Brink, "A Day at a Time," *U.S. News & World Report*, December 1, 2003, p. 52.
36. Quoted in Fox, *Heart Attack!*, p. 89.

37. American Heart Association, *American Heart Association Guide,* p. 187.
38. Steve, personal interview with the author in Las Cruces, New Mexico, November 29, 2003.
39. Quoted in Fox, *Heart Attack!,* p. 113.
40. Steve, personal interview with the author.
41. Brad Henson, *Heart Attack Survivor.* Camarillo, CA: Crow, 2002, p. 124.
42. Henson, *Heart Attack Survivor,* p. 164.
43. Perry, personal interview with the author.
44. Quoted in American Heart Association, "Gerry's Story." www.americanheart.org.

Chapter 5: What the Future Holds

45. Quoted in Michele Meyers, "Red Hot Revelations," *AARP Bulletin,* October 2003, p. 18.
46. Quoted in American Heart Association, "Clotting Protein May Be Link to Heart Disease," October 1, 2003. www.eurekalert.org.
47. Henson, *Heart Attack Survivor,* p. 198.
48. Quoted in *Las Cruces Sun News,* "Research Links Gene, Heart Attacks," November 28, 2003, p. 14A.
49. N.J. Wald and M.R. Law, "A Strategy to Reduce Cardiovascular Disease by More than 80%," *British Medical Journal,* Vol. 326, no. 7404, 2003, p. 1,419.
50. Quoted in Lindey Tanner, "Synthetic Cholesterol Shows Promise for Heart," *Albuquerque Journal,* November 5, 2003, p. A9.
51. Quoted in Jackie Jadrnak, "Cholesterol Cutter Raises Hope," *Albuquerque Journal,* November 17, 2003, p. C1.
52. Quoted in John McKenzie, "Vaccine May Lower Cholesterol," ABC News. www.abcnews.go.com.
53. Quoted in Laura Beil, "Closing Open-Heart Surgery," *Dallas Morning News,* November 25, 2002, p. 10A.
54. Quoted in Beil, "Closing Open-Heart Surgery."
55. Quoted in Avery Comarow and Bernadine Healy, "The Future Is Now," *U.S. News & World Report,* December 1, 2003, p. 41.

Glossary

angina: Temporary chest pain usually caused by exertion.

angiogram: A diagnostic test to check for blockages, in which a catheter with dye is threaded through an artery in the groin up to the coronary artery.

angioplasty: A procedure in which a balloon-tipped catheter is threaded through a blocked coronary artery in order to increase blood flow to the heart.

anticoagulants: Drugs that thin the blood, making it easier for the blood to pass through narrowed arteries.

antioxidants: Vitamins that contain chemicals that prevent oxygen molecules in the body from damaging cells.

arrhythmia: An abnormal heartbeat.

atherosclerosis: The condition of having blocked arteries due to the formation of plaque deposits.

beta-blockers: A type of medication that slows the heartbeat and relaxes the heart and blood vessels.

bioflavonoids: Plant-based compounds that herbalists say dilate the blood vessels.

cardiac care unit: A special section of the hospital used to treat people with heart disease.

cardiac enzymes: Chemicals the heart produces in response to damage.

cardiac rehabilitation: Medically supervised group exercise sessions for recovering heart attack victims.

cardiologist: A doctor who specializes in treating the heart.

cardioplegic solution: A drug used during heart bypass surgery that stops the heart from pumping.

carotid arteries: The two arteries, one on each side of the neck, that carry blood to the brain.

catheter: A small plastic tube.

complementary treatment: The combining of conventional treatment with alternative treatments.

congenital heart disease: A defect in the heart with which a person is born.

coronary artery: A blood vessel that carries blood away from the heart.

coronary heart disease: Heart disease that develops gradually as a result of damage to the coronary blood vessels.

C-reactive protein (CRP): A protein produced in response to inflammation, commonly found in the blood of people with coronary heart disease.

defibrillator: A machine that delivers short, strong electrical jolts to the heart to help restore its natural rhythm.

deoxygenated blood: Blood from which the oxygen has been removed.

echocardiogram: A diagnostic test that uses sound waves to evaluate the ability of the heart to function.

electrocardiogram: A diagnostic test that measures electrical activity in the heart.

fibrinogen: A chemical that promotes blood clots and is often elevated in people with coronary heart disease.

heart bypass surgery: A major surgical procedure that involves the creation of an alternate, or bypass, route around a blocked coronary artery or arteries.

heart-lung machine: A machine that takes over the heart's pumping motion during some heart surgeries.

high-density lipoproteins (HDLs): Proteins that carry excess cholesterol to the liver where it is eliminated; high levels may prevent heart disease.

homocysteine: An amino acid that is often elevated in people with coronary heart disease.

hypertension: high blood pressure

left ventricular assist device (LVAD): A devise that is implanted into a failing heart to help it pump blood to the body.

low-density lipoproteins (LDLs): Proteins that carry cholesterol to all cells in the body; high levels are associated with heart disease.

methionine: A harmless amino acid that homocysteines are converted into before being eliminated from the body.

omega-3 fatty acid: An essential nutrient found in fish that appears to prevent coronary heart disease.

oxidation: The process in which contact with oxygen causes low-density lipo proteins to become sticky.

oxygenated blood: Blood with oxygen in it.

pacemaker: A small electrical device that is implanted into the chest in order to correct a dangerous arrhythmia.

plaque: A hard substance made of cholesterol, calcium, and blood cells that sometimes forms on the walls of coronary arteries.

platelets: Sticky red blood cells that form clots.

saphenous vein: The vein that runs along the inside of the leg that is often removed and grafted on to the coronary artery during heart bypass surgery.

statins: Drugs that reduce cholesterol production.

stent: A small mesh tube that is inserted into a clogged coronary artery in order to keep the artery open.

stress test: A diagnostic test that evaluates the heart's ability to function while under physical stress.

thrombolytic drugs: Medicine that breaks up blood clots.

thrombosis: The blocking of a coronary blood vessel by a blood clot.

vasodilator: A drug that causes blood vessels to relax or dilate.

Organizations to Contact

American Heart Association
7272 Greenville Ave.
Dallas, TX 75231
(800) 242-8721
www.americanheart.org

Provides a wealth of educational material, family health programs, support groups, dietary guidelines, recipes, and research on every aspect of heart disease.

National Coalition for Women with Heart Disease
818 18th St. NW, Suite 730
Washington, DC 20006
(202) 728-7199
www.womenheart.org

Heart news, support groups, patient stories, and information geared toward women with heart disease.

Texas Heart Institute
PO Box 20345
Houston, TX 77225-0345
(800) 292-2221
www.tmc.edu/thi

The largest heart center in the world provides information and health care, and sponsors research about every aspect of heart disease.

Transplant Recipient International Organization
2117 L St. NW, Suite 353
Washington, DC 20037
(800) TRIO-386
www.trioweb.org

This international organization offers information and support for transplant patients and their families.

For Further Reading

Books

John Coppersmith Gold, *Heart Disease,* rev. ed. Berkeley Heights, NJ: Enslow, 2000. A young-adult book that covers the causes, effects, diagnosis, and treatment of heart disease.

David R. Goldman, ed., *American College of Physicians Home Medical Guide to Coronary Artery Disease.* New York: Dorling Kindersley, 2000. Lots of bright pictures fill this book that discusses the symptoms, causes, diagnosis, and treatment of coronary heart disease.

J. Willis Hurst and Jackie Ball, *The Heart: The Kids' Question and Answer Book.* New York: McGraw-Hill, 1999. An easy-to-read book that discusses how the heart and circulatory system work.

Phillip Johansson, *Heart Disease.* Springfield, NJ: Enslow, 1998. This young-adult book discusses the workings of the heart and circulatory system and diseases that affect them.

Web Sites

Children's HeartLink (www.childrensheartlink.org). This charitable organization helps fight congenital heart disease in children throughout the world by sponsoring a number of fund-raising events and providing information.

CongenitalHeartDefects.com (www.congenitalheartdefects.com). Provides support, statistics, fact sheets, research news, and transplant information for people with congenital heart defects and their families.

Congenital Heart Information Network (www.tchin.org). Information, research, and support for people with congenital heart disease and their families. Offers links to summer camps for children with congenital heart disease, chat rooms, and book reviews.

HeartCenterOnline (www.heartcenteronline.com). Offers a wealth of information on every aspect of heart disease, including treatments, lifestyle modifications, and patients' stories.

How Stuff Works (www.howstuffworks.com/heart.htm). Explains how the heart works, how heart disease is diagnosed, and what the disease is.

Works Consulted

Books

American Heart Association, *American Heart Association Guide to Heart Attack Treatment, Recovery, and Prevention.* New York: Times Books, 1996. Gives case histories as examples of what happens before, during, and after a heart attack, and why each event occurs.

Seth Baum, *The Total Guide to a Healthy Heart.* New York: Kensington Books, 1999. Cardiologist Seth Baum provides information on the causes, diagnosis, and treatment of heart disease with an emphasis on alternative and complementary treatment.

Samuel M. Fox, *Heart Attack! Advice for Patients by Patients.* New Haven, CT: Yale University Press, 2002. The book is written from the point of view of heart attack survivors and deals with every aspect of heart disease.

A Healthy Heart. Pleasantville, NY: Reader's Digest, 2000. Provides information about how the heart works, and ways to protect the heart with lots of pictures, diagrams, and charts.

Brad Henson, *Heart Attack Survivor.* Camarillo, CA: Crow, 2002. The author, a heart attack survivor, shares successful techniques that he uses to cope with the challenges of living with heart disease.

Mehmet Oz, *Healing from the Heart: A Leading Heart Surgeon Explores the Power of Complementary Medicine.* New York: Dutton, 1998. Noted cardiologist Mehmet Oz talks about the benefits of complementary treatment for heart disease.

James M. Rippe, *The Healthy Heart for Dummies.* Foster City, CA: IDG Books Worldwide, 2000. Provides a wealth of information about heart disease in a simple, clear format. Also includes a heart-healthy recipe section.

Wayne M. Sotile, *Thriving with Heart Disease: A Unique Program for You and Your Family: Live Happier, Healthier, Longer.* New York: Free Press, 2003. Tips and information about living with heart disease.

Periodicals

Fred Abatemarco, "My Heart Attack," *Men's Health,* September 2002.

Laura Beil, "Closing Open-Heart Surgery," *Dallas Morning News,* November 25, 2002.

Susan Brink, "A Day at a Time," *U.S. News & World Report,* December 1, 2003.

Adam Campbell and Brian Good, "100 Ways to Live Forever," *Men's Health,* July/August 2003.

Avery Comarow and Bernadine Healy, "The Future Is Now," *U.S. News & World Report,* December 1, 2003.

Katherine Griffin, "This Healthy Woman Had a Heart Attack. Could You?" *Good Housekeeping,* October 2003.

Jackie Jadrnak, "Cholesterol Cutter Raises Hope," *Albuquerque Journal,* November 17, 2003.

Las Cruces Sun News, "Research Links Gene, Heart Attacks," November 28, 2003.

Michele Meyers, "Red Hot Revelations," *AARP Bulletin,* October 2003.

Peter Moore, "A Tale of Three Hearts," *Men's Health,* July/August 2003.

T. Rissanen and S. Voutilainen, "Fish-Oil Derived Fatty Acids, Docosahexaenoic Acid and Docosapentaenoic Acid, and the Risk of Acute Coronary Events: The Kuopio Ischaemic Heart Disease Risk Factor Study," *Circulation,* November 28, 2000.

Lindey Tanner, "Synthetic Cholesterol Shows Promise for Heart," *Albuquerque Journal,* November 5, 2003.

N.J. Wald and M.R. Law, "A Strategy to Reduce Cardiovascular Disease by More than 80%," *British Medical Journal,* Vol. 326, no. 7404, 2003.

Internet Sources

American Heart Association. "Clotting Protein May Be Link to Heart Disease." www.eurekalert.org.

———, "Gerry's Story." www.americanheart.org.

Kari Barr, "The Heart of a Mother: Chapter 2, Letting Go," Baby Heart Press. www.babyheartspress.com.

Community Blood Center, "Donor's Baby Benefits from the Community Blood Center." www.kcblood.org.

Deborah L. Dupere, "The Life I Have Lived and Still Live with Heart and Lung Problems," Cardiac Experience Journal, Children's Hospital Boston. www.experiencejournal.com.

Heart Center Online, "Getting My Natural Rhythm Back." www.heart centeronline.com.

———, "My 43 Year Young Heart." www.heartcenteronline.com.

Anna Jaworski, "Growing Up with Congenital Heart Defects," Baby Hearts Press. www.babyheartspress.com.

Dawn Martin, "The Heart of a Mother," Baby Hearts Press. www.baby heartspress.com.

John McKenzie, "Vaccine May Lower Cholesterol," ABC News. www.abcnews.go.com.

Index

Picture Credits

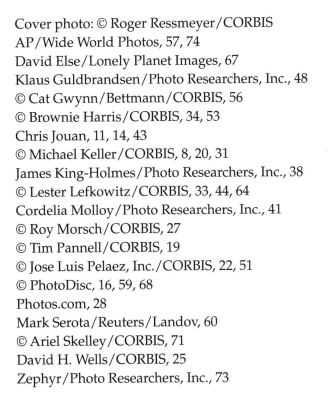

About the Author

Barbara Sheen has been a writer and educator for more than thirty years. She writes in English and Spanish. Her fiction and nonfiction has been published in the United States and Europe. She lives with her family in New Mexico. In her spare time, she enjoys swimming, reading, gardening, walking, and cooking.